D1260525

PRELUDE TO SILENCE

PRELUDE

TO

SILENCE

THE END OF THE GERMAN REPUBLIC

ARNOLD BRECHT

New York · HOWARD FERTIG · 1968

TO THE MEMORY OF

GERTRUD
AND
OSSIP

ERRATA

Page 11, line 4: "84" should read "78"; "1924" should read "1928"

Page 14, line 1: "86" should read "73"
line 3: "63" should read "41"

Page 19, line 13: "ever since" should read "[until 1948]"

Page 28, line 8: "for Cicero" should read "from Cicero"
line 12 from bottom of text: "86" should read "73"; "63" should read "41"

Page 35, line 13 from bottom: "definitely" should read "definitively"

Page 57, line 7 from bottom of text: "Gröner" should read "Groener"

Page 58, line 3: "Gröner" should read "Groener"

Page 69, lines 16 and 17 should be transposed

Page 86, line 7: "Conrad" should read "Konrad"

Page 87, line 13 from bottom: "Supreme State Court" should read "Constitutional Court"

Page 90, lines 8 and 9 of text should read: "When Ebert suspended the guarantees of individual rights for more than a few weeks he included in his decrees a para-" line 6 from bottom should read "Constitution, although it was to stay in force for good."

Page 107, footnote: add "See also *Political Theory,* Princeton, 1959, pp. 117, 159, 207, and 404."

Page 111, line 7 from bottom of text: "such as" should read "though not"

Page 117, line 17: "not care" should read "overlook"

Page 123, footnote: add "See now also *Political Theory,* Princeton, 1959."

Page 127, lines 16 and 18: "vote" should read "votes"
Page 129, footnote: "in 1928" should read "in 1920 and 1928"
Page 151: "Adenauer, Conrad" should read "Adenauer, Konrad"
Page 155: "Gröner" should read "Groener"

Contents

Preface to the 1968 Edition

Prelude to Silence, written in 1943, was published by Oxford University Press in the early spring of 1944, at the height of World War II. The book's reception was mixed at first. While almost all reviews in professional journals and also some of those that appeared in the major newspapers, including *The New York Times* and the London *Times,* were full of praise, other dailies and weeklies denounced the presentation as too favorable to Germany.

Official reactions, too, though outspokenly appreciative of the book's informative value, were rather reserved at first as to the author's interpretation of the events that led up to the downfall of the Weimar Republic. Full disclosure of the Nazi crimes in the early stages of occupation tended to strengthen the unfavorable opinions about the character of the German people as a whole.

By the second year of occupation, however, critical reservations receded. The book's presentation and interpretation also came to be recognized as essentially correct in official quarters. The United States military government even acquired the publication rights for a German translation, which appeared late in 1948 in Vienna (Verlag für Geschichte und Politik) and was well received by German and Austrian papers and professional journals. To both the Americans and the Germans the slender volume became a sort of minor classic in the literature on the collapse of the Weimar Republic.

The American edition has long been out of print. Nevertheless, *Prelude to Silence,* available in public and college libraries, has continued to figure in debates on the causes for the rise of the Hitler regime and to be widely used, so I am told, as a reference in classes on modern history, comparative government, and the theory of democracy. It seems that no other small book has taken the trouble to assemble the data on the constitutional issues involved, the weaknesses of Germany's federal structure, other flaws in the Weimar constitution, the manifold divisions of political opinions in the German people as reflected at the polls, and the final deadlock that led to the disaster, with comparable care, precision, and brevity.

Continuity of demand has caused the present publisher, with the agreement of Oxford University Press, to issue this reprint edition.

Although twenty-three years have passed since this volume was first published, only a few minor errors in figures and other factual statements needed correction. It seemed relevant, however, to add excerpts of a critical letter I received from former Chancellor Heinrich Brüning in August 1944, soon after publication, regarding several controversial points about the period of his chancellorship.

Some of the facts and problems dealt with in *Prelude to Silence* I have treated in more detail in subsequent writings, especially the issues of federalism in *Federalism and Regionalism in Germany, the Division of Prussia* (Oxford University Press, 1945); other constitutional questions in the article "The New German Constitution," in *Social Research* Vol. XVI (1949), pp. 425-73; the problems of dictatorship, totalitarianism, and higher law in *Political Theory—The Foundations of Twentieth-Century Political Thought* (Princeton University Press, 1959); and the entire factual story in my memoirs, recently published in two volumes in German (*Aus nächster Nähe, Lebenserrinerungen eines beteiligten Beobach-*

ters, 1884-1927 [Stuttgart: Deutsche Verlags-Anstalt, 1966], and *Mit der Kraft des Geistes, Lebenserrinerungen zweite Hälfte, 1927-1967* [Deutsche Verlags--Anstalt, 1967]).

But the basic facts, and the drama, are all here.

A. B.

New York, N. Y.
1967

Preface

THIS BOOK RE-TELLS, AND RE-ANALYZES, THE STORY OF THE loss of personal freedom in Germany. More precisely, it describes the political fight in Germany against fascist and totalitarian principles, until their institutional establishment was achieved about half a year after Hitler assumed power. Although there is a good deal of literature on this period, or at least on its first stage, the general and particular story I have in mind has not been related. In part, it has been buried under glossaries and comments of all kinds. Writers in a critical or apologetic mood have focused attention on special events, parties, or persons. Contributing to our knowledge of details they have failed to provide Anglo-American readers with a coherent presentation of fundamental facts. Most narratives end abruptly at some early or middle stage of the fight, leaving the reader at a loss in regard to the events and reasons that led to the final defeat. Writing in retrospect, the authors have not always cared to describe the 'situation,' or, as modern psychologists would say, the 'field' which determined the meaning of events for the actors on the scene, or the conditions that limited the possibilities of action.

In addition, there is a more special factor which has tended to blur the story. Those Germans or former Germans who have been, and as yet are, able to describe the political fight against Totalitarianism and its failure in Germany are themselves more or less victims of the débâcle. A comprehensible state of emotional excitement has caused many to express bitter criticism in almost every direction. The collapse of democracy seemed to require a search for the guilt that caused it. And guilt, apparently, could be found everywhere—in in-

numerable acts and omissions at home and abroad. France
and Great Britain could be blamed for the Treaty of Versailles and its execution, the United States for its repudiation
of the League. At home, the people as a whole could be
blamed, for their historical background, their inherited in-
clinations, their peculiar character, their apathy. Parties and
groups, courts, civil servants, and any number of individuals,
from Chancellors and department heads to advisers and politicians, could be singled out for reproaches. Those responsible
for some details in the Constitution or for the failure to
change them in time could come in for their share of blame
as well as those who initiated certain economic or financial
policies. There seemed to be no limit to possible accusations.
A similar picture has been offered by French refugees after
the collapse of France in 1940.

It is very true, I think, that Hitler's access to power on
30 January 1933 would not have taken place if any of a
number of factors had been different. For this event was
highly accidental in character, if ever there was accident in
history. This is not to say that the collapse of democracy
and the superimposing of some kind of authoritarian government with far-reaching regimentations of many aspects of
life in Germany was a mere accident and could easily if at
all have been avoided in 1932 and 1933. The fact, however,
that it was Hitler and the National Socialist Party with their
fascist and totalitarian principles that took possession of the
machinery of government, and that they could do so the way
they actually did, was made possible only through the con-
vergence of numerous factors. Only a few of these had their
origin in historical trends or in the nature of the German
people. Many were merely accidental.

The accusing formula, so often heard, 'If X had done
(or not done) n at time t, Hitler would not have come to
power,' may therefore be applied rightly to many events.

However, it covers statements of a very different character. X may or may not have been in favor of Totalitarianism. If he was not, the fact that he did (or failed to do) n may imply a fundamental 'guilt' in the sense of an act or an omission that deserves moral condemnation, and such guilt may be anything from a slight neglect to criminal intention. Or the act may have been the result of an 'error in judgment' made in good faith without evil intention and without any neglect of duties and responsibilities. Or it could even have seemed at the time a 'reasonable choice among alternatives.' It makes a great moral difference which of these meanings the statement is intended to have. Even when neglect of duties or responsibilities justifies speaking in terms of guilt, the intention of the agent and his good or bad faith affect the moral judgment in a most fundamental way, placing not only the quantity but the very quality of guilt in a different category.

To make such distinctions does not change the past, but it may influence the future. In fighting Totalitarianism and Fascism we are not only, and not even in the first place, combating individuals and groups, but first of all principles of government which we consider morally objectionable. All those who are seriously opposed to these principles are in some fundamental sense on one side of the line. If in their fight they have made mistakes but in good faith, our language in condemning them should be essentially different from that we use in passing judgment on the principles themselves. The opposite practice, alas! has often been followed. Expressions have sometimes been much more acrimonious in condemning alleged or real mistakes than in denouncing the principles against which the fight was carried on. Many observers, in relating the history of the fight, seem to have their pet enemies among non-totalitarians rather than totalitarians. This indiscriminate condemnation is of no service to the fundamental issue. Nor does it do justice to the German Republic and to democracy in general.

We need a story built around the issue—Fascism and Totalitarianism: Yes or No. A story which discusses the fight with all its vagaries and blunders in a language that distinguishes clearly between adherence to totalitarian and fascist principles on the one hand and the fight against them on the other. That is one of the purposes of this book.

Mistakes, however, will not be minimized. The fact that they were made in good faith will only put them into bolder relief. It is easy to brush aside all lessons by talking of treason. History's greatest lessons are for men of good faith. We have got to learn them lest in spite of good faith we stumble again. The old problems are still with us. They will burst upon the world with the end of hostilities, and most of them are not yet solved, not even in theory. To face them squarely, they must be cleared of anecdotes, ignorance, and hatred.

A number of reasons have made me feel that I could not remain silent in this matter, much as I disliked being distracted from other problems, both general and American, on which I have been concentrating throughout the ten years of my professorship in this country. Few had the opportunity to watch so intimately the history of German Republican administrations from the beginning to the end of the Republic. Fewer still were in a position to do so from so objective vantage points. As this book is not a volume of personal memoirs I am not going to say much about myself. As I shall, however, make a number of statements that are based on my personal knowledge, without referring to any specific source of information, I feel I must give here a few personal data. They are those of a member of the Civil Service who came to work in offices closest to the political events discussed.

When the German Republic was born, I was a counsellor in the Reich chancellery, to which Prince Max von Baden, democratically minded chancellor, had called me only three weeks before, to serve as a secretary to the newly formed quasi-democratic cabinet, i.e. to prepare for the meetings, to take the minutes, and to follow up the execution of the decisions. Eight years of service in the departments of justice and economics had preceded this call. I had begun my career as a judge, and that experience still dominated the pattern of my thoughts and feelings. Remaining in the chancellery when Friedrich Ebert and other commissaries of the people assumed direction of affairs in November 1918, I continued there during the first three years of the Republic with slowly widening functions, which finally, under Josef Wirth and Walther Rathenau, were those of an acting under-secretary. During these crucial years I was present at almost all cabinet meetings, including those in which the decisions on the Treaty of Versailles, on the Weimar Constitution, the fight against reaction and communism, and economic and social policies were made. It was one of my functions to edit the official documents on the events preceding the Armistice. On the night of the Kapp Putsch, March 1920, I was present when Reich President Fritz Ebert and his cabinet left and the usurpers entered. Half a day later, I followed the ministers to Dresden and Stuttgart after handing on to the press the call of the Social Democratic members of the cabinet for a general strike against the usurpers, and after urging the civil servants to refuse active collaboration. The following February, I negotiated at Chancellor Fehrenbach's request with Bavarian nationalists to achieve compliance with the Allies' ultimatum on the disarmament of private organizations. In pursuance of this mission I had discussions with Ernst Pöhner, then president of police in Munich and two years later a leading participant in Hitler's Beer Hall Putsch; and with four fellows handling mailing matter in the backroom of a Munich beer house (a Munich artist took me there), one of whom was Adolf Hitler himself, not yet the leader of his small group at that early time. I discussed affairs also with the papal nuncio, Mgr. Pacelli, later Pius XII, who showed a remarkable understanding for the nationalist reaction in Bavaria because of Munich's experiences with Communist government.

During the following seven years, from 1921 to 1927, I was in charge of one of the three divisions of the Ministry of the Interior, that for constitution, administration, and civil service. There I came to serve in due course under eight ministers—a Social Democrat, a Left Liberal, another Social Democrat (Wilhelm Sollmann, now in this country), a National Liberal (Dr. Karl Jarres, candidate for President in 1925), a German National, two more Liberals, and another German National. I helped draft the Act for the Protection of the German Republic after Rathenau's assassination, and steer it through the parliamentary deliberations. Then I concentrated on constitutional and administrative reforms, in order to make democracy in Germany workable and real. In 1927, the German National minister newly appointed to the department removed me from office at the request of Dr. Hugenberg, his party boss. This step aroused a considerable storm over the Civil Service issues involved, since it was generally understood that it was merely my loyalty to the republican cause that had led to my dismissal. This event thus put a sudden end to the cherished anonymity of an objective-minded expert content to work in the Civil Service for both his country and his ideals.

Only a few days later the Prussian cabinet, still composed of the old Weimar coalition, i.e. Social Democrats, Liberals, and Catholics, appointed me one of their chief delegates to the German second chamber, the Federal Council, especially for matters of the federal budget, and at the end of the Republican period made me their leading representative in that body. During these six years, from 1927 to 1933, I

attended practically all the meetings of both the Federal
Council and the Prussian cabinet, as well as many sessions
of the legislative chambers of Germany and Prussia and of
their committees, while serving simultaneously as a ministerial
director in the state and finance ministries of Prussia. My first
official action happened to be the fight against the appropria-
tion in the 1928 budget for building the first pocket battle-
ship. Federal budget matters kept me in constant touch with
the whole range of Reich politics and with all the leading
personages. This contact was intensified when, from 1928 to
1930, I was made Prussia's representative on the Governmental Commission for Federal Reform, which—presided over by
the three Chancellors of that period and with nine prime
ministers serving for other German states—to a large extent
followed my suggestions. During the subsequent period of
growing unemployment, the Federal Debts Commission, the
administrative council of the Postal Service, and the trustees
of the Public Works Corporation (*Gesellschaft für öffent-
liche Arbeiten, A. G.*) included me among their respective
members.

When in 1932 Chancellor Franz von Papen launched his
coup d'état against the Prussian democratic cabinet, I de-
fended the cause of the Constitution at the Supreme Court.
Thereupon the Chancellor removed me from my offices, but
along with the Prussian ministers I was reinstated by the
Supreme Court. Thus I was back in my seat in the Federal
Council, and was the Council's spokesman, when Hitler was
appointed Chancellor. Re-dismissed a few days later, when
Hitler repeated the 'emergency action' against the Prussian
ministers, I resumed the latters' defense until they abdicated,
and even a little longer. Forced out of my office rooms in the
building of the Prussian Diet by the Storm Troops, I carried
on in rooms of the state ministry. Thus I was literally the
last official in the service of democratic institutions, when I

finally left those rooms on 31 March 1933. Dr. Hans Simons and Dr. Hans Staudinger, now both in this country, Dr. Hermann Badt, now in Tel Aviv, and Dr. Cossmann, still in Germany, were among the last civil servants with me.

A few days later I was arrested 'to protect me from the rage of the Storm Troops,' as the new police president told me—Mr. Diels, whom I had severely attacked in the Supreme Court proceedings. Three points were raised against me, namely: that I had 'supported Jewish immigration' by my votes cast in the Federal Council against a complete ban of such immigration; that I had tried to protect from expulsion a Jewish criminal on parole; and that I had participated in the propaganda campaign against National Socialism. Soon released again, I was prosecuted on the third point because funds under my control had been spent in the fight. The investigation conducted by the new Prussian minister of finance and by the court of accounts cleared me from all charges against my personal integrity. High civil servants in various offices intervened on the ground that I had never acted in contravention to official duties. Although I was declared 'politically unreliable,' they also helped to wrest my passport from Hermann Göring's office and the Secret Police, when finally I left Germany in November 1933 to join the Graduate Faculty of Political and Social Science at the New School for Social Research. It seems that mainly two factors, namely, my long connection with almost all high civil servants and my general aloofness from party politics, were responsible for the assistance I received.

From the foregoing account it will easily be seen that I had unusual opportunities to observe at close hand the fight against Totalitarianism. I do not, of course, claim to have been neutral either in this fight or in that against monarchical reaction and communism that preceded and in part was connected with it. By temperament, by sentiment, by reason, and by loyalty to my sworn duties I was positively on the side of the republican principles of the Constitution at all times, and outspokenly so. Within constitutional limits, however, I did cling to a neutral aloofness from party politics in public life, in line with my convictions in regard to the ideal behavior pattern to be observed inside the Civil Service of a democratic state. Thus I never was a party member, nor did I participate in party campaigns. I even disliked accepting positions that would force me too closely into the politics of individual parties. Five or six times I was asked to accept the office of a permanent under-secretary (*Staatssekretär*) in various departments, including the Reich chancellery under Chancellor Hermann Müller, the ministry of justice under Minister of Justice Koch-Weser, the Prussian ministry of finance, and the Prussian state ministry. Each time I refused, preferring to serve in my independent work, which cut across almost all departmental jurisdictions, as an expert on constitutional, administrative, and financial questions. I knew too well how gravely political and organizational shortcomings blocked productive work of ministers and their under-secretaries. I was deeply interested in working towards a reform of these conditions, especially of the federal system, the electoral method, administration, civil service, public finance, and unemployment policy. This distance from everyday politics tended to increase my independence and my objectivity.

My direct experience in Germany did not end in 1933. Intent on obtaining first-hand knowledge of the situation, my wife and I returned at great risk several times for a few weeks. I trusted to the protection which the closing of the old case against me would give us at a time when the attention of the National Socialists was focused on rebellious party members and conservatives, rather than on former officials and democrats. Thus we were in Berlin during the days of the Blood Purge in 1934, and were spending a vacation in Austria when

Dollfuss was killed. On some other such visit we found a close friend in jail, who was liberated while we were there. Each time I saw scores of old-time friends, in office and out, and visited many sections of the country. Naturally we learned more in a few weeks than strangers could have done in months. All in all, it was a unique opportunity—I know of no parallel case.

Everywhere in this book I have distinguished fascist and totalitarian regimes from all other forms of government, either democratic or authoritarian. In so doing I have used the terms in a definite sense, which I wish briefly to explain.

Fascism, as the term is used here, is always meant to include the following specific feature, namely, that physical force, or the systematic threat of physical force (terror), is employed for the purpose of suppressing any expression of opinions that are opposed to those either held or tolerated by the fascist group. It is characteristic of Fascism that such terror is applied both through individual and mass demonstrations of force, and that the use of physical compulsion is glorified as a principle superior to the principles of discussion and peaceful persuasion rather than excused as a regrettable measure applied in an emergency.

The term Fascism is best suited to designate these principles, as it was formed purposively from the Latin word *fasces,* signifying bundle of rods, and was meant to carry the connotation 'You'd better obey, or we'll beat you up until you do.' In contrast, the term National Socialism is highly misleading if used to designate fascist principles. Some national kind of socialism may be far removed from any glorification of violence. In fact, there was a 'national-social' movement under the leadership of the eminent democratic politician Friedrich Naumann in Germany, adherents of which are among the German refugees. I therefore prefer using the term

Fascism for all phenomena of the type described above, and I shall speak of National Socialism only when reference is made to the specific National Socialist German Workers' Party, which has become the vehicle of Fascism in Germany.

Fascism is different from Communism not only because there is a great difference in aims for the attainment of which violence is used, but also because Communism, much as it has applied physical force in practice, does not glorify its use. It may make no difference to the person who is being beaten up or otherwise brutally treated whether this procedure is glorified as a higher principle or is used for other reasons and perhaps with regret. In the conflict between ideas, however, the issue is markedly different in the two cases.

Totalitarianism refuses to acknowledge any limitation on what the government is entitled to do in order to reach its proclaimed purposes. Both Fascism and Communism may be totalitarian, while Humanism, Democracy, and true Christianity, as well as the other great religions, can never be. For, however much they may differ in other parts of their messages, they are at one in recognizing ethical limits to governmental action, and hold that the dignity of man ought to be respected in every human being.

'Totalitarian democracy' is a contradiction in terms. Even if the majority in a democratic country should go far in using 'total' means to reach their purposes, e.g. victory in war, they recognize that there are ethical and institutional limitations to their use of power, or they cease to be democratic. To illustrate, it is of the essence of democracy that a country may determine its legislative and executive representatives by the free use of the franchise, either directly or indirectly. This principle cannot be completely abandoned, unless the country gives up democracy. On the other hand there are brands of authoritarian government, too, that are neither fascist nor totalitarian, such as constitutional limited monarchies. Even absolute monarchy is not totalitarian if the monarch recognizes the law of God or ethical principles as binding on him.

The distinctive use of terms is necessary in order to conduct an orderly discussion. This does by no means preclude the argument that any authoritarian government is dangerous because it carries the risk of a turn to Fascism or Totalitarianism; or that democracy may degenerate into anarchic stages which in turn may engender Fascism and Totalitarianism— arguments as old as Plato and Aristotle. Investigations of what elsewhere I have called the 'implied risks' of governmental systems are most fertile for political discussions.[1] They cannot, however, be carried through fruitfully unless the meanings of the concepts used in the discussion are clearly defined.

In concluding, I wish to acknowledge the stimulus which this book owes to the fact that in 1942 Professor Carl Joachim Friedrich of Harvard asked my co-operation in the plan for a collective book on the fight in all its stages against Totalitarianism in Germany. The contributions that could be collected at present on the period after the establishment of Totalitarianism were too episodic and uneven to offer an adequate picture, however, and they often involved danger for persons still in Germany. The completion of the plan had, therefore, to be postponed. Meanwhile the essay that was to form the first part grew and finally became this little book. It may now serve as an introduction to the studies that are forthcoming from the research project on Germany in Post-war European Reconstruction, conducted by the Graduate Faculty at the New School for Social Research.

I wish also to thank Gertrude Marburg and my unforgettable friend, the late Louis Marburg of Montclair, N. J., who,

[1] See 'The Impossible in Political and Legal Philosophy,' *California Law Review*, vol. 29 (1941), pp. 312, 323.

while I have been writing this, gave me the freedom of American farm life in the small country town of Hamburg, N. J.; and Maude A. Huttman, formerly Professor of Modern European History at Barnard College, who not only has been indefatigable in watching over my English, but whose constructive criticism and suggestions have inspired me much beyond the technical aspects of this essay.

This book, however, is dedicated to the memory of two of those whom we longed most to see whenever we returned to Germany. It cannot harm them any more if I mention their names. On our last visit, in July 1939, we found my beloved sister, Gertrud, unconscious in a Berlin hospital. For three days we sat at her bedside, until life had flown from her strong heart, and her face had assumed the features of a saint, beyond suffering. She had decided to end her life together with her husband, Ossip Schnirlin, a great violinist and musician, of Jewish descent, who succumbed before we arrived. Up to the end of 1938 both had carried on with great courage and with an almost superhuman patience, concentrating on 'real' values—those of the human soul, as expressed in music, in great poetry, and in the signs of true friendship they received to their very last day. During the spring of 1939 his nerves had come to fail him under the constant mental torture. He was determined to die rather than wait for what might happen. When she saw that she could no longer hold him back, she chose to go with him in order to make it easier for him. We had come to plan with them for their future. We were too late by one day.

A. B.

New York, N. Y.
February 1944

NOTE

The courtesy of Doubleday, Doran and Company, Garden City, New York, in permitting quotations from Herbert Hoover and Hugh Gibson, *The Problems of Lasting Peace*, is gratefully acknowledged.

Translations from the German are by A. B., unless stated otherwise.

Introduction

Three Stages of a Fight

THE FIGHT AGAINST NATIONAL SOCIALISM IN GERMANY HAS run through three main stages. The first covers the time before Hitler became Chancellor; the second, the period up to the suppression of all political parties except that of the National Socialists half a year later; and the third, the time thereafter.

The conditions and the character of the fight in these three stages have been very different. During the first period, it was conducted under a democratic constitution against an anti-democratic movement. Natural leaders on the democratic side were the cabinets and parties in power. They had at their disposal the official machinery of law enforcement, of public education, numerous newspapers, free speech and free assembly, and they could embark on any political counteraction that was in line with the principles of tolerance and respect for individual rights as guaranteed in the Constitution.

The struggle in this early period, therefore, was fundamentally different from that in its third, the totalitarian, stage, in which any plan that offered the slightest aspect of active opposition to National Socialism came to be considered a violation of the law of the land, and to expose the planner to crushing blows by the governmental machine. In their defense of the regime the new authorities were no longer hampered by constitutional limitations of ends or means, or by ethical regard for the dignity of the individual. The official syllogism of right and justice was based on the two premises that right is what is useful to the German nation, and that National Socialism *is* useful to the German nation. It followed, then, by mere inference, that right is what is useful to National Socialism. This principle has determined the rules of the game ever since the third stage was reached.

Between this totalitarian phase of the struggle and its beginnings under the Weimar Constitution there was a period of about half a year that differed from both the other two. It was characterized by the 'sliding' form of the National Socialist revolt, i.e. by its legalistic disguise, which made it impossible to ascertain a definite date on which the Constitution was violated. How far Hitler's power would extend was a matter of conjecture. Many observers entertained doubts about his personal intentions. There was a certain possibility left for political opposition to assert itself. The opponents of Totalitarianism made attempts to get control of the regime by a variety of means, such as imposing legal limitations on Hitler's power, or using the authority of old Field Marshal von Hindenburg, or arranging for effective political combinations to check one-party rule, or by promoting evolutionary tendencies within the party and thus splitting off their radical wing. While such endeavors were carried on by those who had still some freedom of action, numerous victims of party squads and unofficial gangs had to fight for their lives, many of them falling prey to acts of terror or vengeance. Simultaneously, the great exodus started of those who saw no opportunity for action left in Germany. The struggle in this second period was, therefore, conducted as it were on several levels.

Much as the methods have varied, at all stages and levels the German people have shown more fighting spirit than is generally recognized outside Germany. Only a small portion of the heroes and victims in this fight are known, while most of them will be unknown forever. This, in the third stage, is due to the complete control of communication and publicity by which the regime has prevented concerted action against itself in Germany ever since it assumed total power. This control has reached much further, and much deeper, in Germany than it ever has in any of the occupied countries, with the exception of Austria. Perfect knowledge of the language in all its variations, of localities and habits, has made it possible for the Gestapo,[1] and for party members supporting the police, to control any undesirable communication or conspiracy that went beyond whispering discussions among a few friends. Abroad, the Gestapo have been unable to go so far, not only because their lines thinned considerably with expansion, but more especially because as foreigners, even if they had some command of the language, they were unable to get the meaning of communications—oral, written, or over the telephone—with the many forms of allusion and disguise that can be used to mislead foreigners. Nor could they know the many places where secret gatherings might be held, and the means of access or escape. Only where they relied on a considerable force of native support had they any chance of tightening their control to a degree approximating that applied at home.

In Germany, however, control grew so strict that any fights which did occur were doomed to remain those of isolated individuals or small groups. The general public in Germany did not even hear of them, except in some instances when the regime could not prevent the news from spreading or when it thought it proper to refer to them. Those few who escaped to foreign countries could tell abroad but not in Germany what they had suffered, seen, and heard.

While this explains the dearth of news about the fight against Totalitarianism in the third stage, it obviously does

[1] Gestapo is the official abbreviation of *Geheime Staats Polizei,* meaning the state's secret police.

not account for the victory of the regime during the first and second stages. Why, then, do we know so little about the fight of those who loved freedom, *before* National Socialism assumed full control? Was there no fight? Were there no lovers of freedom?

I

Have Germans Always Been Totalitarian?

Political Composition of the German People

THE APPARENT APATHY WITH WHICH THE GERMAN PEOPLE
seemed to accept National Socialism in 1933 has fostered the
opinion that the great majority of Germans were either National Socialists themselves, or predisposed to condone if not
to embrace totalitarian doctrines because of their political or
intellectual heritage. The democratic period is, according to
this opinion, explained as a mere episode, as an anomaly, fundamentally incompatible with the characteristic traits of the
German people; an artificial product, evolving from defeat
and from the pressure exerted by the Allies in 1918 in favor
of a democratic reorganization in Germany. According to
this view the Germans severed bonds with authoritarian traditions only in order to obtain better peace conditions and
merely for the time being. They remained at bottom, so it
was said, as they had always been, monarchists longing for
military splendor, violence, expansion, command, and obedience.

There are indeed many indications that the democratic
form of government, at least in the peculiar incarnation it
had found in Germany, was unpopular with considerable
portions of the people. It would, however, be rash to con-
clude that these oppositional or wavering groups were inclined towards fascist principles. Numerous election returns
showed that this was not so.

Even if the first elections after the November revolution

of 1918 may have failed to reflect the people's true sentiments accurately, because at that time external considerations may have caused the voters to cast their ballots for parties that did not express their real views, there is little reason to believe that the subsequent elections also were not indicative of popular opinion. Freedom in the electoral system, extension of suffrage to all men and women from twenty years onward, secrecy of the ballot, freedom of speech and of the press, of assembly and association, and the hardships under which the people were suffering, made it very unlikely that their votes were cast in contradiction to popular sentiment. Nor is it correct to assume that the distribution of votes during the democratic period showed a sudden difference from that in monarchical elections. On the contrary, there was a remarkable continuity.

General, secret, and direct elections were held for the German Reichstag since 1871. Campaigns and their results, therefore, revealed the main currents of thought and the relative strength of parties long before postwar tactics could have played a role. The last elections to the Imperial Reichstag, held in 1912, are most illuminating for the present purpose. Of 397 seats, as many as 110 fell to the Social Democrats, 91 went to the Catholic Center, and 42 to Left Liberals. These three groups, all deeply opposed to principles that now would be called fascist, mustered therefore 243 out of 397 members, that is almost two-thirds of the house. Of the remainder, 28 represented minorities, i.e. Poles, Alsatians, or Danes. They were, of course, opposed to German nationalism or racism. Farther to the right, the 45 National Liberals, although Bismarckian in traditional views, were sincerely devoted to some fundamental principles of liberalism, such as independence of judges, religious tolerance, and international trade, and can therefore not be claimed for Fascism. Beyond

these various groups there were at the right of the Reichstag
no more than 47 Conservatives, 13 Free Conservatives, 3 Anti-
Semites, and 8 members of an Economic Union Party, together 71 out of 397. A few Hanoverian Autonomists and
Independents account for the remaining 10 seats.

The Socialist-Catholic Majority

The post-war Reichstags show striking similarity of composition to the last pre-war Reichstag. This is particularly
evident with the Social Democratic and Catholic Center parties. In 1912 the number of Social Democrats had already far
outstripped that of the various conservative parties. Their
number would have been even higher had not gerrymander-
ing and the system of run-off elections worked to their dis-
advantage. Actually every third voter (34.8 per cent) elected
a Social Democratic candidate in 1912. This was not a sudden jump, but rather the result of a gradual advance. Every
fourth voter (27.2 per cent) had given his vote to a Social
Democrat as early as 1898.

There was no spectacular change in this ratio after defeat
and revolution. In the elections to the National Assembly of
January 1919, 163 out of 421 seats went to Social Democrats
and 22 to Independent Socialists, together 185. Although
these figures signified a further increase, the decisive step
from one-third of the voters to the majority was not achieved.
Nor was it ever achieved later. Throughout the whole democratic period the share of votes for the Socialists remained
above one-third and short of one-half of all votes cast.

The bulk of these votes always went to the Social Democrats, who were strictly democratic and anti-communistic;
the remainder, at first to the Independent Socialists, and later
to the Communists. Let us consider only the last elections:

Members elected	1928	1930	1932 (July)	1932 (Nov.)
Social Democrats	153	143	133	121
Communists	54	77	89	100
The two Socialist parties together	207	220	222	221
All parties together..........	491	577	607	584

The aggregate of the Socialist members was always more than one-third; never did it reach one-half of all members of the Reichstag. Even in March 1933, in spite of the grave terroristic pressure applied against them, the Social Democrats obtained 120 and the Communists 81 seats, together 201 out of 647. This was, for the first time since 1919, less than one-third, but not a great deal.

No less indicative is the share of the Catholic Center Party in both the old and the new Reichstag. The Roman Catholics in the greater part of Germany have been a religious and political minority ever since the Reformation and the religious wars. Distinct from their Spanish and French cousins they lived in opposition to monarchical authority in protestant principalities, which discriminated against them in various ways and sometimes put them to a hard fight, as during Bismarck's *Kulturkampf*. They therefore came to stress freedom of worship and civil equality of citizens against authoritarian rule. Whatever their views may have been in regard to other questions, there can be no doubt that Germans who gave their votes to Centrist candidates were opposed to totalitarian plans and in favor of the preservation of the basic principles of Christianity.

It is amazing to see how little the number of Centrist members in the Reichstag varied during the whole period from 1871 to Hitler's access to power. There happened to be 91 of them in the Reichstag of 1874, in that of 1912, and in the

National Assembly of 1919. When the Bavarian section of the party formed a separate group under the name of Bavarian People's Party, both together retained about the old strength, ranging from a low of 84 members in 1924 to a high of 96 in July 1932. They were still 92 in March 1933, 74 of whom belonged to the Old Center, 18 to the Bavarian Catholics. The percentage that went to the Catholics of all votes cast in Germany declined slightly from 16.4 in 1912 to 15.0 in November 1932. But they always maintained a high place among the parties both absolutely and relatively.

Adding up only the figures of Socialists, including the Communists, and Catholic Centrists, we find a majority of the German people in patent opposition to fascist principles from periods prior to the First World War to the end of the democratic period. For their combined votes represented the majority of the votes cast in every election to the German Reichstag from 1912 to 1932 inclusive, although sometimes only by a narrow margin, as in the first election of 1924 and both elections of 1932. Locally their preponderance remained strong even then. In the northern part of the Rhineland (electoral district of Cologne-Aachen) they polled together 73.6 per cent in November 1932 and 62.4 per cent even in March 1933. Only 17.4 per cent of the votes were cast for Hitler in this district in November 1932, and only 30.1 per cent in March 1933, despite the terror exercised at the time.[1]

The Liberals

To these figures we must further add those of the liberal bourgeoisie. There were 42 Left Liberals in the Reichstag of 1912 and 75 in the National Assembly of 1919, when they experienced their boom as the Democratic Party after the Revolution. This boom proved illusionary, it is true. The

[1] Westphalia, too, and even Berlin had less than 35 per cent National Socialist votes still in March 1933, although Berlin had few Catholics.

number of their seats was reduced to 39 in 1920 and to 25 in 1928. Yet there doubtless was a genuine liberal wing in the German bourgeoisie down to the end of the 1920's. Nor is it permissible to count all of the National Liberals, Stresemann's party, among those who had totalitarian tendencies. Their number had been 45 in 1912 and, under their new name German People's Party, was the same again in 1924 and 1928 after a drop to 19 in favor of the Democratic Party in 1919, and a brief upswing to 65 at their cost in 1920.

The final attrition of the two Liberal parties—the Democratic and the German People's Party—began in 1930, when they obtained only 14 and 30 seats respectively. It continued in 1932, when they aggregated no more than 11 members in July and 13 in November, and in March 1933, when their combined membership dropped to 7. One reason for this attrition was the system of Proportional Representation, which favored the rise of various interest groups instead of a general liberal party. These groups cannot generally be considered as susceptible of totalitarian views. Other parts of the Left Liberals were obviously attracted to the Social Democratic Party. A considerable number of the younger generation, especially of new voters without jobs, seem to have found their way to the National Socialists. Yet figures show clearly that this was a *novel* development, and marked a breach with liberal traditions. These sections of the German people had not been 'always totalitarian.' They had been definitely anti-totalitarian in the past and they had expressed their traditional convictions faithfully down to the end of the 'twenties. Whatever the causes of their defection from liberalism, they were in conflict with the liberal evolution of more than one hundred years.

The Reactionaries and the Fascists

This analysis of the German people prior to 1930 is further confirmed when finally we turn to the Right proper. In the 44 German Nationals of the 1919 National Assembly we can easily discover the successors of the 71 Conservatives, Free Conservatives, Anti-Semites and the like of the 1912 Reichstag. Their number had dropped to a low of 10.5 per cent of the total. Yet they had not mustered more than 17.6 per cent before the First World War. There is no surprising breach in continuity. That may seem astounding in view of the manifest influence that the Conservatives exercised in imperial Germany. Figures demonstrate clearly, however, that this influence had not been founded on numerical strength. It was based on the fact that the Constitution of 1871 made the emperor independent of the Reichstag in the selection of the government personnel in civil and military services. It was for this reason that offices were filled with Conservatives. Social Democrats were completely absent, and few Liberals and Catholics could be found in politically important positions. Furthermore, the Conservatives were numerous in the Prussian Diet, which continued to be elected under the most reactionary system down to the fall of the monarchy. In studying the Germans at that time it is necessary to turn one's eyes from those in power, to the people. There the conservative outlook was restricted to a small portion.

That portion grew in the 'twenties in opposition to the Treaty of Versailles, to democracy, and to inflation. Under a new name, the German Nationals, they regained 71 seats in 1920, corresponding to the combined seats of Conservatives and their associates in 1912. They grew even to 96 and 103 in the two elections of 1924 after the inflation period, not counting the 32 and later 14 'Racists' (Anti-Semites) that made their separate appearance in these elections. Thereafter they dropped to 86 in 1928, now flanked by 12 National Socialists, who replaced the Racists. Gains by the National Socialists brought them further down to 63 in 1930 and 37 in July 1932. In November 1932, when the National Socialists lost 34 seats, the German Nationals obtained about half of them, raising their number to 51. This number they could hold, and even improve by one, in March 1933, after they had climbed on to Hitler's band wagon. Even at their height in 1924, however, they did not reach even one-fourth of the membership of the Reichstag. They could be glad as a rule if they mustered about 15 per cent of the votes at the polls.

The National Socialists had no considerable number of followers up to 1930. There were, as just mentioned, 32 'Racists' in May 1924, reduced to 14 in December of that year, as there had been a small group of Anti-Semites in the imperial Reichstags from 1887 to 1918. In their stead, 12 National Socialists appeared in the Reichstag of 1928. This was all they could achieve, although Proportional Representation secured them seats according to their voting strength, there being no possibility as in France, Great Britain, and the United States of crowding extremist candidates out by local combinations against them. Not until September 1930 did the National Socialists show a considerable backing.

In view of these facts and figures and their continuity nothing can be more devious than the opinion that the Germans have always been totalitarian and that the democratic regime served only as a camouflage to conceal this fundamental fact. The overwhelming majority of the people at the end of the imperial period and during the democratic regime were distinctly anti-totalitarian and anti-fascist in both their ideas and their principles. This remained so at least throughout the 1920's.[2]

[2] See Appendix A, The Fallacies of Intellectual History, and Appendix B, The Weakness of Democratic Cabinets in Germany.

II

The Twenties—Fight Against Fascism

Does Not Figure

Democracy's Original Foes

IT IS AGAINST THIS BACKGROUND THAT WE MUST STUDY THE question of the fight against Fascism through the main period of the German Democracy. Among the various shades of opposition against the democratic form of government the National Socialists played a very minor role close to 1930. Outside Bavaria there seemed to be no need for a serious political fight against a group that revealed so little numerical strength. Their principles and claims appeared hollow and crazy to most political leaders as well as to the great majority of the voters, and not worthy of serious refutation. Even if Italians had succumbed to such silly and cruel theories, so ran the usual argument, it was ridiculous to think that any large number of Germans ever would.

The fight in defense of democracy, at that time, focused on Communists and German Nationals, both of whom mustered considerable strength. Much as the Weimar coalition parties differed in their views, they were united in their opposition to those two major parties that wished to discard the basic principles of democracy. That, no doubt, both of them wanted to do: the Communists, by establishing the dictatorship of a section of the proletariat, the Nationalists, by freeing the executive branch from parliamentary control. Yet by no stretch of the imagination would it have been possible to describe the views of the German Nationals as fascist at that time. They were generally adherents of a return to a constitutionally limited monarchy, similar to that which had been in existence from 1871 to 1918.

That regime, it is true, was distinctly undemocratic in form as well as in spirit. It was, however, far from being fascist and totalitarian. Legislation and financial measures depended on the consent of the popularly elected Reichstag. The courts were fairly independent, and almost all the individual rights that are commonly connected with the idea of a democratic bill of rights were guaranteed by statutes that could not be altered without the Reichstag's consent. Respect for ethical and religious values and for the dignity of man was recognized as a leading principle of government. The most reactionary part of the governmental structure existed in Prussia, where the three-class franchise kept the number of Socialists and Liberals down and secured a reactionary majority. But even there people were by no means under a fascist rule, since federal legislation determined the rights of citizens. Independent courts could be appealed to in any case of violation of the law. Within twenty-four hours any arrested person had to be brought before the ordinary court, which could set him free if the facts failed to warrant his detention. Freedom of the press was guaranteed by a federal law of 1874, and freedom of association and assembly by another, most liberal, federal act of 1908. This was no Fascism.

Rarely did wishes of the Rightist parties during the 'twenties go beyond the restoration of that pre-war constitutional picture. Many would have accepted slight modifications, such as the restriction of the monarchical apex to one monarch instead of the many territorial princes from of old, or would even have condoned a republican presidency. Much nearer to Totalitarianism were the Communists, who for the purpose of thorough socialism frankly preached the abolition of general elections and of individual rights.

Kapp Putsch, Inflation, and Beer Hall Putsch

Although the main adversaries of democracy were no fascists at that time, great personal courage was required in the daily fight for democracy. Communists resorted to the use of terror from the Left; *Freikorps* (patriotic volunteers), secret organizations, and clubs from the Right. The number of those killed during the first two years after the war was considerable. The reactionary Kapp Putsch of March 1920 led to the surprise occupation of great parts of Germany, including Berlin, by rebellious groups. Only the grim determination and the disciplined fighting spirit of the workers could overthrow them. Yet the workers were not alone in that fight. Although at first caught napping, the democratic cabinets of the Reich and of Prussia, under the active leadership of the first President of the Republic, Friedrich Ebert, were strong and unwavering in their measures of defense. They were supported by the bulk of the Civil Service under the lead of the permanent under-secretaries, who joined in the defense by a formal statement and by refusing to co-operate with the usurpers. Thus by the combined counteraction of the legitimate chief executive, the federal cabinet and the state cabinets, party leaders, civil servants, and workers, the rebel government was manœuvered into surrender within a week.

Those rebels were no fascists. They were Conservatives and generals of old-fashioned ideals. Nor did they apply fascist methods in order to terrorize reluctant civil servants into submission. To a certain extent they tried to maintain 'gentlemen's standards' during their revolt. The National Socialists later blamed them for their moderation and ascribed to it their failure. They studied the story of the Kapp Putsch closely.

Communist uprisings were the natural aftermath. After their bloody suppression, pacification seemed to have been achieved. But uprisings flared up time and again. The first prominent victims of Rightist attacks were Matthias Erzberger in 1921, who had signed the Armistice, and in the following year, Walther Rathenau, foreign minister, who had inaugurated the 'policy of fulfilment' with regard to the reparation debt. It may be recalled here that Rathenau was convinced the debt could not be paid, yet he had reached the conclusion that nothing but the sincere effort to pay it would demonstrate the impossibility to the Allies. These and others were victims of what we may now call fascist methods. Yet there was no distinct fascist philosophy in Germany at that time. The assassinations could be interpreted, and were interpreted, as acts of a misled patriotism such as have occurred elsewhere in similar situations. Carried out by immature youths, they were not approved even by the reactionary parties. Political excitement, natural after a long war and its unhappy ending, could explain violent outrages and could induce the governments not to generalize their significance.

Such interpretation was also given to the first conspicuous action of the young Hitler movement, namely, the Beer Hall Putsch in Munich, which led to his arrest and that of his followers. At that time, November 1923, the hectic period of inflation had reached its peak. The dollar, quoted at 400 marks in July 1922, and 4,000 marks four months later, was 4,000,000 marks in August 1923. It jumped to 4,000,000,000 in October and 4,000,000,000,000 in November of that year, i.e. at the time when the Putsch occurred. Treasury bills bore designations of trillions of marks. Daily food sold for billions. Wages lagged behind, although they, too, reached ten and thirteen figures for the week. People lost their savings. The printing press was unable to keep pace with the daily demands for the ever new units of treasury bills. It was not surprising that strange things happened during such a collapse.

The young Republic survived the crisis. Although the reactionary governments in command in Bavaria had entertained encouraging relations with the extreme movements of the Right and had failed to check Hitler up to the last minute, they finally did check him, and sent him to prison.[1] In near-by Saxony, a semi-Communist government which had gone to the other extreme was deposed by a Reich Commissioner equipped with extraordinary powers based on dubious presidential authority. In Berlin, Stresemann as Reich Chancellor had succeeded in forming a 'Great Coalition' that reached from the Social Democrats to the National Liberals, the party of big industry and finance. His cabinet was finally able to stabilize the currency, if only at the rate of one trillion marks for one reichsmark, the new unit, which has ever since remained in force in Germany. Although the different treatment meted out to the Saxon and Bavarian governments caused the Social Democrats soon to leave the coalition, peace and order were gradually restored.

The Beer Hall Putsch seemed to be only an episode in this inflation crisis, not to be taken too seriously. The reactionary Bavarian Government released the imprisoned leaders after a year, during a period of relative calmness and slight recovery. The National Socialist Party, dissolved for a time under an emergency law, lived on as a 'movement.' It lent its votes to a combination of various anti-semitic groups, which obtained 32 seats in the Reichstag elections of May 1924, but only 14 in that of December of the same year, after the Reichstag had been dissolved for the first time under the Republic. This remained their reduced strength for four years. The next regular elections, in 1928, kept the representation of the National Socialist Party down to only twelve.

[1] See Appendix C, State Police Power and the National Socialist Party.

Presidential Election

The two elections of 1924, while leaving the fascist candidates in a position of relative unimportance, gave the German Nationals remarkable strength. The number of their seats grew to 96 in the first election of that year, and to 103 in the second. For the first time since the Armistice they assumed a share of responsibility by entering cabinets together with the Catholic Center and the National Liberals, tolerating even Otto Gessler at the head of the defense ministry. He was a non-parliamentarian classed as a democrat and, whatever else he may have been, was certainly neither totalitarian nor conservative. The new German-National members of the Reich cabinet had to swear allegiance to the Republican Constitution before they could take office. Although such co-operation on the basis of the Constitution aroused some hope for a progressive acceptance of parliamentary forms, it implied a swing to more conservative ideas.

This shift in emphasis was strengthened when Field Marshal von Hindenburg was elected President of the Republic after Ebert's death in 1925. There were two ballots. In the first, in which Hindenburg was not yet a candidate, more than seven candidates competed. The Social Democrat, Otto Braun, received 7.8 million votes, the Catholic Centrist, Dr. Marx, 4.0 million, the Liberal, 1.6—together 13.4 million votes cast for candidates of the Weimar Coalition parties out of a total of 27.3 million. A separate candidate of the Bavarian Catholics polled one million votes. The candidate of the joint Rightist parties, Dr. Jarres, a National Liberal mayor, obtained 10.8 votes, while the special candidate nominated by the fascist and anti-semitic groups, General Ludendorff, received only 0.2 million. In addition, 1.9 million votes were counted for the Communist candidate. There was no fascist touch that could have frightened anyone, in these results.

The relative majority lay clearly with the left and middle parties. The German Constitution required an absolute majority on the first ballot. No candidate having reached that majority, run-off elections were to be held, in which the relative majority would decide the election. Hindenburg, put forward as a new candidate of the joint Rightist parties, profited from four factors. These were: his own popularity; the fact that many people prefer non-partisans to leaders of parties other than their own; the obstinacy of the Communists in supporting a separate candidate; and finally the unwillingness of many Protestants to vote for a Roman Catholic, i.e. for Dr. Wilhelm Marx, who had been chosen as the candidate of the joint Weimar Coalition parties.[2] (The experience of Alfred Smith, a Catholic, in a presidential election in the United States offers some analogy with that of Dr. Marx.) Hindenburg polled 14,656,000 votes, Dr. Marx, 13,752,000, and the Communist, Thälmann, 1,931,000. Hindenburg's victory over the candidate of the democratic parties was, therefore, by a small margin and possible only because the Moscow-instructed Communists in their blind fight against all parliamentarian parties insisted on casting their votes for their own candidate instead of throwing them into the balance against the nationalist candidate. After all, there was much that was accidental in the result.

For a short while the outlook was gloomy indeed for liberal and democratic ideas. Although there was no fear that a fascist regime might be established, there was a real concern lest some kind of a constitutional limited monarchy might be restored. Hindenburg soon dispelled these apprehensions. He took the oath of allegiance to the Weimar Constitution. In a statement which he made between the two ballotings for the presidency he said: 'If duty should command me to act

[2] Wilhelm Marx, then leader of the Catholic Center Party, has no connection with Karl Marx, founder of Marxian Socialism.

as Reich President I shall not fail to disregard all differences of party, person, origin and profession, as the Constitution requires.' As a matter of fact he did abide strictly by the Weimar Constitution with dignity and conscientiousness through the whole seven years of his first term in office.

III

1930—The Fight Starts

The Great Coalition

THE REICHSTAG ELECTIONS OF 1928 RESULTED IN A CLEAR DE-
feat of the German Nationals, who now had only 73 seats
instead of 103, with a few more seats for split-off groups of
agrarians. The leading opposition party, the Social Democrats, increased their representation from 131 to 153. The
National Socialists obtained only 12 seats, while the Communist numbers had grown from 45 to 54. The middle parties each lost a few seats.

The swing of the pendulum to the left was so clearly
marked that the Center-Right majority, including the Catholics, National Liberals, and German Nationals, which had
formed the cabinet during the last year, could not continue
in office. For the first time since 1919 the parties of the
Weimar Coalition—Social Democrats, Democrats, and Center
—approximated an absolute majority in the Reichstag. Yet
they were short of it by six seats. A so-called Great Coalition
cabinet, therefore, was formed. Under the chancellorship of
the Social Democratic leader, Hermann Müller, it included
Social Democrats, Liberals (Democrats), Catholic Center,
and National Liberals (German People's Party), with Gustav
Stresemann of the latter party continuing as foreign minister.

This cabinet, with minor changes, held office for two
years. Its main concern was the lightening of the unbearable
international burdens. The domestic fight still was directed
against the German Nationals and the Communists rather

than against the few National Socialists. The National Socialists' motion for a vote of censure against Stresemann in
November 1928 was rejected by 219 against 98 votes. Even
when in October 1929 Stresemann died, and was followed in
office by his friend, Julius Curtius, there was at first no fundamental change. At the end of November the Reichstag rejected with 318 against 82 votes the adoption of a bill that
forbade the cabinet to sign the new covenant on the reparation debt, known as the Young plan. The popular referendum
held for the same purpose on 22 December drew less than
14 per cent of the voters instead of the more than 50 per cent
needed for its adoption. In the course of events the German
Nationals split, and their moderate wing formed a distinct
party, the Conservative People's Party. The cabinet seemed
to have the situation well in hand. While political passions
over the Young plan ran high, while frequent clashes in public
meetings and even bomb plots occurred, the main domestic
conflict still was one among the major political parties rather
than between the government and the fascist group. In January 1930 the Young plan was signed. In March the Reichstag ratified the treaty with 266 against 193 votes.

Unemployment Crisis

Meanwhile, however, unemployment had become a major
issue, which led to a split in the cabinet. To understand the
political crisis that was occasioned by the rapid growth in
unemployment one must recall that the doctrine of 'compensatory government spending' had hardly been conceived and
was certainly not well established anywhere in the world at
that time. This doctrine, which later led to the conspicuous
development of the Work Projects Administration in the
United States, recommends that governments in a period of
depression should finance public works with borrowed
money, even if the projects are not self-liquidating, and holds

that such additional government spending will have no inflationary effects so long as unemployment has not been absorbed. In 1930, there was still the general fear that additional government spending of borrowed money *would* lead to inflation, unless it was restricted to self-liquidating projects. This fear was particularly strong in Germany, where the horrors of the runaway inflation of 1923 were still in everybody's mind. Nor was borrowing on the credit of the nation as easy there as it was in the United States. It often appeared impossible to float even small government loans for unobjectionable purposes in the open market. To provide hundreds of millions, or even billions of marks for non-self-liquidating projects, it would have become necessary to print additional paper money, or to extract fictitious loans from government-controlled institutions, or to invent brand-new methods of financing that had never been tried. There were several proposals offered to that effect. The Communists recommended the Soviet method. Yet that presupposed acceptance of a totalitarian economic system. The National Socialists, too, had only proposals that involved the establishment of totalitarian methods in complete abandonment of the free market in domestic and international trade. There were also a few proposals that aimed at providing money for public works without having resort to such extreme methods, one of which will be mentioned later.

It was none of these proposals that led to the crisis of the Great Coalition. The cabinet was agreed that retrenchment of expenditures on the one side and additional taxes on the other were necessary in view of the increase in relief expenditures and the rapidly dwindling revenues. On the details, however, the ministers were unable to reach agreement. Should cuts in unemployment-insurance benefits and relief rates also be considered? The trade unions said No, and they prevailed on the Social Democratic Party to accept their view. The other parties said Yes, and Hermann Müller and his Social Democratic friends in the cabinet, with the exception of Rudolf Wissell, minister of labor, were willing to compromise with them. Yet the unyielding attitude of the parliamentary parties—with both the National Liberals and Social Democrats opposing any compromises, and Stresemann, who might have mitigated the conflicting views, dead—blew up the cabinet just as the British Labour cabinet exploded one year later on the same issue.

There was, however, this difference. While the British Prime Minister, Ramsay MacDonald, left the Labour Party and stayed in office to carry through his plan of retrenchment in a national coalition cabinet, the German Chancellor, Hermann Müller, although equally opposed to the opinion that prevailed among the majority of his party, left office and stayed in the party. The Great Coalition collapsed. The result was the birth of a minority cabinet, formed by Heinrich Brüning, the budget expert of the Catholic Center. While MacDonald's defection from his party led to the formation of a strong parliamentary majority in England controlled by the Conservatives, Hermann Müller's loyalty to his party left Brüning at the head of a minority. Although taking the moderate Conservatives that had separated from the German Nationals into his cabinet, Brüning had to rely on additional support either from the Social Democrats or the Right from case to case and could be confronted with a vote of censure any day.

Recourse to Presidential Powers

Despite its weak basis the cabinet embarked on its policy of retrenchment and taxation with a great deal of energy. When its proposals failed to find a majority and no adequate alternative that would have been supported by a majority seemed to be available, Brüning resorted to presidential legislation by decree. The emergency powers of the President, never thus far used by Hindenburg, but often by Ebert in the first, the hardest, period of the Republic up to 1924, were constitutionally well established. The authors of the Constitution thought that they had sufficiently safeguarded these powers against anti-democratic abuses. Presidential emergency decrees required the countersignature of the Chancellor or other ministers, whose terms of office could be terminated by a vote of censure in the Reichstag, and any such decree had to be repealed whenever a simple majority of the Reichstag so demanded.[1] The Reichstag in the present case did so demand. Brüning complied, but appealed to the people by causing the President to dissolve the Reichstag. Pending the elections he issued new decrees.

This was the great chance of all opponents of parliamentary democracy. They could refer to the fact that a policy which the government held indispensable could not be carried through by parliamentary means. Simultaneously, they could exploit the natural opposition of all receivers of salaries, wages, pensions, unemployment-insurance compensation and relief, against cuts in these payments. They could blame the 'weak international policy' of the democratic cabinets for the economic crisis, the world-wide nature of which was not yet recognized, and which even when understood could easily be charged to the Versailles Treaty.

Moreover, in connecting the dissolution with the issue of new decrees Brüning set a most dangerous precedent. His intentions undoubtedly were pure. Others after him, however, could—and actually did—refer to the precedent he had established, when they applied the same technical methods for the purpose not of saving but of destroying democracy. It thus could be literally said of his action what in the year 63 B.C. the young and still inconspicuous senator Julius Caesar said

[1] See Appendix D, on Article 48 of the Weimar Constitution.

to Cicero, then consul at the height of his power, when the latter applied a death penalty of dubious constitutionality to five followers of Catiline:

All bad precedents have originated in cases which were good; but when the control of the government falls into the hands of men who are incompetent or bad, your new precedent is transferred [to the punishment of] the undeserved and blameless . . . For my own part, I fear nothing of that kind for Cicero, but in a great Commonwealth there are many different natures. It is possible that, when someone else is consul, some falsehood may be believed to be true. When the consul with this precedent before him shall draw the sword . . . who shall limit or restrain him? [2]

The Great Surprise

Although the advantages the opposition could draw from the situation were widely felt, the practical results came as a surprise to all. While on the Left the number of Communist members jumped from 54 to 77—as had been expected by many—it was not the German Nationals of the Right who gained. They were reduced from 86 to 63 members, and even the National Liberals from 45 to 30. However, the National Socialists returned with 107 members in lieu of their old twelve. This meant an increase of more than 800 per cent.

No one had foreseen such figures. Brüning would hardly have dissolved the Reichstag if he had. The Reichstag as elected in 1928 could have continued for two more years. The National Socialists had hoped for only 40 to 50 seats.

Spectacular as their sudden jump in votes was, the National Socialists still represented only a minor fraction of the people. In none of the 35 large election districts of Germany had

[2] Sallust, *The War with Catiline*, translated by J. C. Rolfe, Loeb Classical Library, pp. 95, 97. The scene has been ably described by H. J. Haskell, *This Was Cicero* (Alfred A. Knopf, New York, 1942), p. 192.

they polled as much as 30 per cent of the votes, and only in one—Schleswig-Holstein—more than 25 per cent. Not even had they local majorities anywhere in the country. A recent analysis by F. A. Hermens has made this point clear.[3] As he has shown, there was no majority of National Socialist voters in any of the 400 smaller districts that Germany might have had under some one-man-district system of elections, such as that used in the United States, Great Britain, France, or imperial Germany. In no such district did they poll more than 40 per cent of the votes, and only in 23 more than 30. In the vast majority of single-man constituencies their share would have been far below 20 per cent. If the American or British plurality system of elections, which gives the seats to the candidates with the relative plurality of votes, had been in force in Germany, the National Socialists would have had no chance of gaining more than 10 or 20 seats, if that many. Nor would they have fared better under the French and imperial German systems, with their run-off elections, which tended to unite the moderate parties against the extremists.

The truth of this analysis notwithstanding, the result of the elections brought National Socialism into the political limelight. We may, therefore, speak from now on of a political fight against Fascism, as essentially distinct from the fight against the nostalgia for a return to constitutional limited monarchy. It is important to realize that this new fight had its starting point as late as the fall of 1930, or shortly before, and that one would look in vain for it much earlier, except in local happenings, especially in local conflicts between Communists and National Socialists.

If one were to write a history not of the fight against National Socialism but of the causes that made its rise possible,

[3] *Democracy or Anarchy?* With an introduction by C. J. Friedrich. Notre Dame: The Review of Politics, 1941, p. 259. See also Appendix B of this essay.

he would of course have to start much earlier. The war, the sudden collapse after what appeared to Germans as 'a thousand victories,' and the mistakes made in the treatment of the republican German cabinets by the Allies from the Treaty of Versailles on would all figure large in that story. Another chapter would have to deal with the defects in the Weimar Constitution, of which we shall speak later. One could further blame the domestic governments for mistakes made in the handling of such problems as inflation. One could point to the unwarranted credulity of the Rightist parties who helped the National Socialists along in the hope of being able later to control them, or to the short-sightedness of the Communists, who by their radical fight against all democratic cabinets and candidates made the victory of the National Socialists possible. In the list of tactical mistakes, the failure of the parties to continue the Great Coalition in 1930 and Brüning's dissolution of the Reichstag in a psychologically dangerous moment would have to bear their share of the blame. Finally, the economic crisis and unemployment and their causes and potential cures would fill pages of such an analysis.

All these facts, and many others, have something to do with the rise of Fascism in Germany. A goodly number of people can claim that they were engaged in passionate combat to prevent each of these facts from materializing. That combat, however, was not yet directed against Fascism. The fight against Fascism did not begin to be a major political issue prior to the fall of 1930. Even then it was still far from being in the center of politics.

IV

Fighting Fascism by Fighting the Economic Crisis

Growth of Unemployment. The Financial Gap

ACTUALLY, THE ATTENTION OF THE BRÜNING CABINET WAS focused on the economic and financial crisis and on foreign affairs rather than on the growth of the National Socialist Party. To overcome that crisis seemed to be the primary task. Without its successful solution, chaotic conditions were sure to develop, resulting in dictatorial experiments of either the extreme Left or the extreme Right. Success would bring victory over National Socialism in its wake. Whatever objections may be raised against the adequacy of Brüning's economic plans and the methods by which he carried them through, no one can justly deny that he was right in thinking that the national government should take the initiative in the fight against the economic crisis and that this was also the most effective weapon in the fight against totalitarian plans.

Germany's economic and financial situation was indeed desperate and seemed about to collapse completely. Rising unemployment swelled public relief expenditures, while public revenues lagged far behind. The United States, too, has known grave unemployment and sharp drops in revenues. Yet the situation in Germany became much worse than it ever grew here. While out of 10 trade-union members less than 1 had been unemployed in 1928, more than 2 were so in 1930, more than 3 in 1931, and more than 4 in 1932. These figures do not include those who had part-time jobs. When

31

4 to 5 out of 10 were fully unemployed, 2 to 3 were partly so, and only 3 were fully employed.

Despite the severe cuts which Brüning carried through by decree, and the introduction of the means test after six weeks of unemployment insurance compensation, the total amounts, federal and others, that were spent to meet unemployment increased from 1.2 billion reichsmarks in 1928 to more than 3 billion in 1932, not including sums spent on public works. At the same time, federal revenues dropped from 9.3 billion reichsmarks in 1928 to 6.6 billion in 1932, despite some ten additional taxes by which the Brüning cabinet tried to keep the coffers filled. Among these additions was an increase in the federal sales tax from .80 to 2 per cent; the abandonment of the refund of income taxes deducted at the source that had been granted in case the final return did not justify the deduction; a flat poll tax, and several other additions to the income taxes; a new salt tax; the doubling of the sugar tax; and the capital-flight tax. But all these additions did not prevent that drop in revenues of almost one-third.

Deflation Policy, Tolerated by the Reichstag

For the reasons set forth above there was no possibility of bridging, by government loans, a remaining gap of 4 billion reichsmarks between revenues and expenditures. Even small loans for capital outlay in current budgets could not be floated. Month after month, the cabinet was kept in a state of excitement about the possibility of providing the necessary cash for the pay rolls of public employees and for the statutory contributions to the expenditures of states and municipalities. More than once loans could only be obtained under humiliating conditions. Shortly before Brüning's appointment, the under-secretary in the national ministry of finance, Johannis Popitz, had informed the state governments that he might be unable to transfer to them their due portions of the income taxes. They protested against having the deficiency thus passed to them.

This calamity of the public finances was increased by the threatened collapse of the great private banking institutions in July 1931. To avert it, the federal treasury was forced to intervene. This implied assuming additional financial burdens.

To avoid the 4 billion gap, the cabinet gradually cut down expenditures by about one-third of the 12 billion expended in 1928. Half of this reduction was made possible by the cancellation of the reparation debt, prepared in long and consistent negotiations. The other half was effected, in the main, by a rigid curtailment of salaries and pensions. They were cut down by 19 to 23 per cent in three steps: first, 6 per cent, on 1 December 1930; next, an additional 4 to 8 per cent, 5 June 1931; finally, a further 9 per cent, 8 December 1931.

To make these cuts in the salaries of public employees effective also in states and municipalities, and correspondingly to curtail the federal contributions to their expenditures, Brüning had to go far in using all possibilities offered by Article 48 of the Weimar Constitution, providing for presidential decrees in an emergency. To mitigate the effect of these cuts on living standards he had further to use presidential emergency powers for cutting down prices. But he duly placed each decree before the Reichstag, ready to repeal it if a majority should so demand, and to resign if he was defeated on an essential question or if a vote of censure was passed.

Faced with totalitarian threats from Left and Right, the Reichstag reconvening after the elections of 1930 tolerated, although often reluctantly, Brüning's 'constitutional dictatorship.' Fifty decrees were issued, many of them of considerable length. Thirty-eight of them bore on economic and financial questions. The Reichstag did not ask for their repeal, or pass a vote of censure. Frequent motions from the Opposition that repeal should be demanded obtained no majority. The Social Democrats, although often disinclined to vote positively for the measures, abstained from voting for their repeal, because this would only have led to a new parliamentary crisis. Their positive vote was not required. The National Socialists withdrew from the meetings of the House, when they saw that their parliamentary opposition was of no avail.

Error, Guilt, or Reasonable Choice?

It has become more than doubtful whether Brüning's deflation policy was wise. To cut Germany's cost of production about 20 per cent and thereby to give German exports that much of a competitive advantage on the world market might have been called a sound plan from the merely economic point of view, except for the inherent danger that it could be counteracted by action in other countries. Actually, Great Britain did meet this challenge to her trade effectively by three countermoves, i.e. by devaluating the pound sterling by more than 20 per cent in September 1931; by reducing the salaries of public employees by 10 to 15 per cent in the same month; and by introducing protective tariffs in 1932. These three measures gave her export trade more than the equivalent of the benefits Germany had derived from hers. The United States tightened its protective tariffs as early as 1930. Therefore, on the international market Germany's great effort was widely deprived of its hoped for fruits. Domestically, the various cuts in salaries, wages, pensions, unemployment compensations, and relief constantly irritated and increasingly antagonized all those who received such payments, and made them the easy prey of anti-democratic propaganda, the more so as the regime rested on legislation by decrees. The soundest economic measure becomes unhealthy when it upsets the political balance and throws the country into the turmoil of revolt and revolution.

Some critics have gone so far as to blame Brüning's economic policy for everything that has befallen Germany and the world thereafter. They ought to weigh their words carefully, so as not to confuse error in judgment with moral guilt in so great an issue. Many mistakes have been made since 1918 and before, by many statesmen in many countries, and many of these mistakes can be stigmatized as steps along the road that led to ruin. Rarely have errors in judgment been committed with a cleaner moral conscience than were those of Brüning's cabinet. This is written by one who at the time ardently opposed the unemployment policy, but who is willing to remember that not only was the theory of compensatory spending then still in its infancy, but also that the difficulty in placing government loans and the popular fear of runaway inflation were serious obstacles in Germany.

The Record. On the Threshold of Salvation

The results achieved by the cabinets of Müller and Brüning from 1928 to 1932, if measured by their aims and purposes, were of the highest order. Subsequent events should not be allowed to detract from this fact. The Allied Forces of Occupation left the Rhineland definitely in 1930, five years before the originally stipulated term had expired. The Agent General for Reparation Payments with his staff departed. So did the other Allied commissions of control that had been set up under the Versailles Treaty. The cancellation of Germany's reparation debt was underway, so that appropriations for that purpose in the current budget could be omitted. If the Disarmament Conference had not yet led to a definite result, an agreement that either Germany should be permitted to double her military strength or the other major powers should cut down theirs, or both, had been so near acceptance that a final decision could soon be hoped for. The general atmosphere in international quarters was more favorable to

Germany than it had ever been since the War. Domestically, the monthly anxiety of the ministry of finance, whether there would be cash enough for meeting current obligations, was a thing of the past. The budget was well balanced. The federal debt was extremely low, totalling about 14 billion reichsmarks, i.e. 3.5 billion dollars at the current rate. The total of all the federal deficits of the past not yet cleared on Brüning's exit from office was considerably under 2 billion reichsmarks. Count Schwerin von Krosigk, the finance minister under Papen and Hitler, explained on 11 January 1933 that this state of affairs could be regarded with great satisfaction.[1] He referred to the fact that the deficits of the United States and France had each been about five times higher in a single year. A potent Public Works Corporation, authorized to give self-liquidating grants-in-aid to states, provinces, counties, and municipalities for public works, had been created and functioned satisfactorily. Future financial operations on a large scale would have a sound basis. The collapse of the great financial institutions had been avoided, mainly by a system of federal outlays and guarantees rather than by direct contributions. This again had been made possible as a result of the rigid financial principles applied by the Brüning cabinet everywhere.

This record might have counted for much in the fight against Fascism, if there had been time to utilize it for the cause of republican government. However, the crisis in unemployment was not yet overcome. Rather it had grown throughout the whole period. After having disposed of the other great problems, the cabinet could have concentrated on it. It seemed easier after the financial situation had so much improved and the reparation debt was about to be cancelled

[1] He had been the head of the budget division in the ministry of finance under Brüning's chancellorship. Brüning's minister of finance was Hermann Dietrich.

to expand the public works program. The democratic Prussian cabinet, in a letter from cabinet to cabinet written at Easter 1932, and through its representatives in the Reichsrat, urged Brüning to go ahead. If money was not otherwise obtainable, they recommended cutting down the hours of work temporarily so that the majority of the unemployed would be absorbed, even if that should mean a temporary resort to a 32-hour week. The large amounts saved on unemployment-insurance benefits and general relief, together with any other amounts that could be raised by financial transactions, should then be used to finance public works.

But there was no time left to carry out these or other plans. Brüning found himself out of office a few weeks before the international conference met that had been called to consummate the cancellation of the reparation debt. The beneficiaries of the great work done in international and financial affairs were Papen and Hitler.

How close the democratic policy had led to an agreement on even the thorniest of all problems, that of armaments, is best illustrated by the following quotation from Herbert Hoover and Hugh Gibson, *The Problems of Lasting Peace*.[2]

When the Disarmament Conference met in Geneva in 1932, it was obvious that the German attitude would determine the possibilities of success. Chancellor Bruening took the ground, at once enlightened and practical, that Germany wanted to contribute toward creating a situation where there could be a general reduction of armaments He did not ask to be relieved of Part V of the Treaty of Versailles, under which Germany was completely disarmed, but suggested some unimportant changes which would have lessened the sense of humiliation and inferiority and would have enabled him to turn the thoughts of Germany away from their sense of grievance to more constructive tasks. The American, British, and Italian governments saw his proposals as

[2] Garden City, N. Y., Doubleday, Doran and Company, 1942, pp. 167-8.

opening the way to possible success, but the French Government, clinging to the letter of the bond, declined even to discuss any suggested changes in the treaty, maintaining that the Germans had made a bargain—that they must stick to it.

Chancellor Bruening stated at the same time that he felt the greatest contribution that Germany could make to the general cause of disarmament would be to shake off the sense of grievance which might lead to an attempt at forcible revision of the Treaty of Versailles. He was convinced that this was just as much in the interest of Germany as of the other powers, but saw clearly that if there was to be no relaxation even in the appearance of the military clauses, there was the danger that demagogues could stir up a sense of grievance which would lead to dangerous results. His forebodings were only too well founded. Only a few months after his proposals had been scornfully rejected, Hitler came to power, largely upon the indignation he had been able to arouse in Germany over real and fancied grievances. And liberal government in Germany was destroyed.

Here we have another example of the inadequacy of concessions made too late. As soon as Hitler came to power, the French Government manifested a quite different attitude and made a series of proposals which would have been more than adequate while Bruening was in power. Greater and greater concessions were offered by France and rejected by Hitler. And even in France there was a considerable feeling that if Chancellor Bruening had been met in a reasonable way, and helped to dispel the sense of wrong and humiliation, it is highly improbable that Hitler would have succeeded in gaining mastery of the government. The failure to act reasonably on this matter contributed to the success of the Nazi party, with all its disastrous consequences.

Of the two writers, the one was President of the United States at the time, the other, chairman of the American delegation to the Disarmament Conference of 1932.

V

Fighting Fascism by Frontal Attack

Prussia in the Fight

THE FIGHT AGAINST FASCISM WAS OF COURSE NOT ONLY ECO-
nomic, nor was it only concerned with the improvement of
foreign relations. It was also a fight for democratic law enforcement against anti-democratic lawbreakers. Enforcement
under the Weimar Constitution was primarily a matter for
the several states, however, and not for the federal government. In this respect, the federal power was unduly weak.
Unless the national government resorted to presidential emergency decrees, it had to rely on the good will and the ef-
ficiency of the state governments. This was in striking contrast to the United States, where federal legislation may be
enforced through federal courts and federal police.

As enforcement policy depended on the views of the state
governments, it varied from section to section. In Prussia it
was definitely democratic. The Prussian cabinets included
members of all three Weimar Coalition parties continuously
from 1919 to 1932, even at times when the Reich cabinets
excluded Social Democrats and Left Liberals in favor of
National Liberals and German Nationals. This picture, which
so strangely differed from that of imperial times, resulted
from the fact that Social Democrats, Left Liberals, and Catholic Centrists polled a slightly larger share of the popular
vote in Prussia than they did elsewhere, as for instance in
Bavaria, Saxony, Thuringia, Brunswick, Oldenburg, and
Hamburg, where either parties further to the Right (includ-

ing the Catholic 'Bavarian People's Party') or Communists, or both were relatively stronger. Thus there was no need of abandoning power in Prussia for the democratic parties, and when the Social Democrats left the national cabinet, they still kept their seats in the Prussian. The offices of both the Prussian prime minister and minister of the interior—the latter being in charge of police matters—were held by Social Democrats throughout Brüning's national administration. The Prussian minister of justice—who proposed the appointment and promotion of judges, and supervised the state attorneys—was a member of the Catholic Center, like Brüning himself. Fundamental questions of law enforcement were, of course, discussed in the entire cabinet, and all measures were subject to criticism in the Prussian Diet, which had the power to change the composition of the cabinet.

Democratic principles of tolerance, and in particular the constitutional clauses guaranteeing freedom of speech, assembly, association and of the press, set limits to what the states could do in the exercise of their police power. They could not, for example, apply preventive measures, such as prohibiting in advance meetings and publications. Nor could associations be disbanded, unless their *purpose* was demonstrably directed towards the violation of the law. Individual violations committed by members of an association were not sufficient cause to warrant its dissolution. Suspension of constitutional guarantees could give the state governments wider authority. Such suspension, if any, could issue only from the federal government, or with its approval.

It is not easy to prove that the 'purpose' of an organization is directed toward violation of the law, if the leaders know how to express themselves carefully enough. The troops of the Communists, the so-called 'Red Front,' were disbanded in 1929 in Prussia, as they had been in Bavaria earlier, and the Supreme Court confirmed the constitutionality of this order. In view of the evasive nature of the National Socialist propaganda it was doubtful, however, whether the courts would confirm a similar measure also against the National Socialist Party or its formations, which were disguised as protective guards. These doubts increased, when Hitler in September 1930—during proceedings against three Reichswehr officers who had engaged in forming National Socialist groups within the Army—made a sworn statement in court that he was now pursuing his goals along strictly legal roads only. Thus the Prussian cabinet waited for the Reich cabinet by a presidential emergency decree to disband the Storm Troops throughout the entire Reich. This could not be challenged in court on the ground of the constitutional right of freedom of association, because Article 48 authorized the President to disregard that freedom in emergency decrees.[1]

Meanwhile, the Prussian police concentrated on the prevention of actual outbursts of violence and on the prosecution of individual extremists who violated the law. In addition, the Prussian cabinet took three steps in 1930. It issued directions that neither National Socialists nor Communists should be granted the approval of the state government as required by law, if they were elected to municipal offices, such as that of mayor. (Ordinances of 31 January and 3 July.) It also decided that civil servants, i.e. *Prussian* civil servants, must not be members of either party. (Ordinance of 25 June.) It further forbade the wearing of uniforms by members of the National Socialist Party and of its sub-groups. (Ordinance of 11 June.)

In sum, Prussia was strongest among the German states in her anti-fascist measures for law enforcement. Bavaria led in pursuing a more lenient practice. Thuringia, in February

[1] See Appendices C and D regarding the details.

1930, and Brunswick, in September, went even further in accepting National Socialists in their cabinets.

Unless the state governments clearly violated federal law, the national government had no regular constitutional power to interfere with their police practices. Short of taking over the administration of police into national hands by virtue of Article 48—a decision certain to lead to grave conflicts, especially with Bavaria—the federal government could only use indirect means. It sometimes did so. Thus, when the National Socialist Wilhelm Frick became Thuringian minister of the interior, the Reich cabinet refused to pay federal grants-in-aid for the Thuringian police, until compliance with the federal legislation was secured. As to the number of people concerned, Thuringia and Brunswick were of little importance, however, since they included less than 4 per cent of the German population. Such was the situation of law enforcement which the national cabinets had to consider.[2]

Brüning in the Fight

The increasing threat of violence and terror caused Brüning to take a hand in the frontal attack against extremists. Decrees to this effect were issued in March, July, August, October, and December of 1931, and again in April 1932. They ordered that the police had to be given 48 hours advance notice of all public meetings in the open air, and of parades; that such meetings and parades could be forbidden if facts substantiated the fear that public peace and safety would be endangered; and that political posters, tracts, and propaganda sheets had to be shown to the police first, who could forbid their dissemination, when necessary to protect public peace and safety. They banned the use of trucks in political parades, because trucks had often served as armored

[2] Appendix C contains further illustrations.

cars. They expressly authorized the state police to ban private uniforms and badges of political organizations, because the legality of the Prussian ban, which had been issued without special authorization, was questioned by the highest court; and they later (November 1931) issued such a ban directly to the entire realm, thus prohibiting the wearing of Brown Shirts in public everywhere. They also authorized the police to shut down gathering places where acts hostile to the Weimar Republic or dangerous to public peace and safety had occurred. They increased the penalties for high treason committed against the Republic, and for omitting the names of editors and of the printing press on publications that contained treasonous passages or that in other wise broke the rules laid down for the preservation of public peace and safety. They ordered the police, if necessary for the maintenance of peace and safety, to arrest and detain any person who was caught wearing arms where that was forbidden, such as in public meetings and parades. The person arrested could appeal to a judge only on the question whether he had violated the law. If he had done so, he could not dispute his detention up to three months.

All these decrees were signed by President von Hindenburg when the Brüning cabinet presented them to him. They supplemented the Protection of the Republic Act, which had first been passed long before Hindenburg's election, and later had been prolonged for two years in 1927 and re-enacted with some modifications in 1930 over his signature. This statute had already fixed penalties for certain acts preparatory to assassinations or to the overthrow of the constitutional form of democratic government, and all abusive language employed deliberately and in bad faith against it or against the republican flag or colors. It had also authorized the state ministries to suspend, for four weeks, the publication of any newspaper in which such violations of the laws were found,

allowing however an appeal to the Supreme Court. Constant
increase in terror and violence had caused Brüning to propose
the additional measures mentioned above, and Hindenburg
gave them his signature.

The disturbances had become grave indeed. In the majority
of cases the clash was between National Socialists and Communists. Yet collisions with defenders of the Weimar Constitution also led to casualties. Month after month, numbers
of persons were killed in rows or were dastardly slain. In
February 1932, for instance, eight were killed, three Communists, three National Socialists, and two others. In March,
eleven died violent deaths. Nine were Communists, two National Socialists. In April, six were killed—three Communists,
two National Socialists, and one other; in May, seven, four
of whom were Communists and two National Socialists.

Hindenburg in the Fight and His Re-election

At that time new presidential elections were due. The
enormous tension and the pending solution of great foreign
and economic questions convinced the cabinets of the Reich
and Prussia that they should not try just then to change the
incumbent of the highest office. Hindenburg had been beyond
reproach faithful to the Constitution. Although remaining
conservative in his basic ideas, he had never refused to act
according to his constitutional duties. Hitler was a pied-piper
candidate. It was felt sure that Hindenburg could beat him,
but not so sure that some other candidate could, or that the
parties would agree on somebody other than Hindenburg.
Once sound conditions on the labor market were re-established and the current international issues finally settled, old
Hindenburg might retire and a new President be looked for.
But swapping horses while crossing the stream was not to be
recommended, so it appeared to most advisers.

There was not the slightest reason at that time to doubt

Hindenburg's continuing the fight against National Socialism. It was not alone Brüning who thought so as he campaigned for Hindenburg. The Prussian prime minister, Otto Braun, who had been the Social Democratic candidate for President seven years before, issued a campaign proclamation for Hindenburg, in which he contrasted him with Hitler:

Embodiment of tranquillity and steadfastness [*Ruhe und Stetigkeit*], of manly loyalty and devotion to the fulfilment of his duties towards the entire people; whose life lies open before everybody's eyes; who has shown, and by no means least so during his seven-year term as Reich President, that all those can rely on him who want to deliver Germany from chaotic conditions and lead it upward, out of her economic misery, in peaceful co-operation of all classes, bound together in a common fate . . .

I am separated by a deep gulf from Hindenburg in my world view and political standpoint. Yet the human factor [*das Menschliche*], which unfortunately counts little today in public life, has built across that gulf a bridge that has brought us together, uniting us in the desire, each according to his convictions, to promote the welfare of the people. I have come to know the Reich President as a man on whose word one can trust, a man of pure intentions and detached [*abgeklärt*, i.e. matured, ripened], filled with a Kantian sense of duty, which has caused him once more to place himself at the German people's disposal and to assume the heavy responsibilities of his office, in spite of his high age and his comprehensible yearning for rest.

With this proclamation [3] Otto Braun in full accord with the Social Democratic Party threw the 7 to 8 million votes that had been cast for him seven years before, to Hindenburg, who obtained 19.4 million votes against Hitler's 13.4 and the Communist's Thälmann 3.7, in the run-off elections of 10 April 1932.

Braun's description was considered correct by almost

[3] Published in *Vorwärts*, 10 March 1932.

everybody. The Social Democratic historian of the German Republic, Friedrich Stampfer, writes (*Die vierzehn Jahre der ersten deutschen Republik*, Karlsbad, 1936, p. 563): 'Otto Braun met with no contradiction, either openly or covertly, when he wrote: "I have come to know the Reich President as a man on whose word one can trust." Everyone regarded Hindenburg as such a man.' He refers to the fact that Hindenburg himself said in his campaign speech that he had accepted the candidacy 'to prevent the election of Hitler,' whom he called an advocate of 'one-sided and extreme views.' He, Hindenburg, would rather be misunderstood and personally attacked than 'knowingly let our people, who have suffered so heavily during the last one decade and a half, run into new civil fights.'

And indeed, three days after his re-election, Hindenburg took up the frontal attack against Fascism in line with his previous policy. At the recommendation of Brüning and General Gröner, minister of defense and of the interior, he signed a decree ordering the complete disbanding of the Storm Troops of the National Socialist Party.

VI

Fighting Fascism by Constitutional Reform

Fatal Points in the Weimar Constitution

TAKING THE WEIMAR CONSTITUTION AS A WHOLE, IT WAS from the democratic point of view a document worthy of veneration. But the haste in which it had been composed, its authors' lack of experience, the absence—not only in Germany but also elsewhere in the world—of advanced political theory with regard to several problems of greatest importance, and furthermore, the reassuring presence of a first President, Friedrich Ebert, whose deep adherence to democratic principles was beyond any doubt, led to the incorporation of a few fatal clauses. The following three mistakes proved particularly grave:

(1) Proportional Representation, unfortunately guaranteed in the Constitution, prevented the integration of diversified views.[1] It strongly promoted the splitting up of parties. Worse, it led to the nomination and election of representatives who were stalwart group delegates rather than personalities trained and able to find a compromise among various groups, interests, and views. Worst of all, it made it impossible to build up local combinations that could outvote extremists. The low age qualification of twenty years for voters helped to swell the number of ballots cast for extremist groups.

(2) Presidential election by popular vote, while satisfactory under a two-party system, is bound to be a most danger-

[1] See Appendix B.

ous method wherever there are numerous and disintegrating parties. If no party is able to get its own candidate elected, the natural result is the nomination of popular outsiders who are political laymen lacking strong affiliations with any parliamentary party. Had the election of the President been left to a joint meeting of the two houses, as in France, Hindenburg would not have been even a candidate after Ebert's death, and the election of a genuinely democratic parliamentarian would have been secured.

(3) The presidential powers were not limited carefully enough. That the President should obtain broad emergency powers under parliamentary control was perhaps inevitable in the complicated situation of postwar Germany. As long as the countersignature of the cabinet and the right of the Reichstag to demand repeal were realistic checks, the emergency powers were not in themselves objectionable. The loopholes for authoritarianism were rather to be found in the unconditional terms by which the President was given the right to appoint and dismiss the Chancellor. According to the broad formulation of this clause, a Chancellor could be dismissed even before he was defeated in the legislature, and one who had little chance to obtain a vote of confidence could be appointed and could countersign presidential orders to dissolve the Reichstag as well as presidential emergency decrees, the repeal of which the Reichstag, if dissolved, was unable to demand pending elections. The emergency decree powers could therefore pass into the hands of persons not controlled by parliament. This was the more dangerous as these powers included the right to suspend all habeas-corpus privileges of persons arrested or detained by the police. No minimal guarantees for the limitation and control of police practices in such cases were embodied in the Constitution.

These mistakes [2] relate only to a few lines of the long con-

[2] See Appendices B and D for details.

stitutional document. Yet their influence on the fate of the German Republic proved to be preposterous. It is not too much to say that, if they had not been written into the Constitution, the history of Germany would have taken a very different course, although it may be impossible to say exactly what that course would have been. The truth of this sweeping contention becomes evident when one considers the enormous impulse that Communists as well as National Socialists obtained from their large representations in the Reichstag, which they would not have had under another electoral system. It is clear too that old Hindenburg could not have played his particular role in the shift to Fascism if the President of the Republic had been elected in the French way by the two houses. Then Hindenburg would not have been elected. Under a democratic President there would have been no opportunity for a 'sliding' revolution under legalistic disguise. It was, as we shall see later, this disguise which paralyzed the faithful adherents of the Constitution in their fight against Hitler, because they did not want to be the ones to violate the Constitution. Again, if the rights of the President had at least been more carefully limited, Hindenburg could not have dismissed Brüning in 1932, nor could he have appointed Papen, or dissolved the Reichstag with the latter's futile countersignature, or removed the Prussian ministers, or suspended individual rights with no guarantee left for even the most fundamental elements of justice and humanity.

Why Some Defects Were Not Corrected

Mistakes made in a written constitution are hard to change, once it is adopted, whenever the distribution of 'power' is the issue. Up to April 1932, the second and the third defect in the Constitution, i.e. the dangers inherent in the presidential elections and presidential powers, seemed to exist only in theory and not in practice. Neither Ebert nor Hindenburg had ever abused the full powers granted them in appointing and dismissing Chancellors. Hindenburg had avoided using Article 48 throughout the first five years of office. He had only resorted to it at Brüning's request and then under parliamentary control. People are not easily persuaded to change a constitution for theoretical reasons. A two-thirds majority in both houses was required for amendments. Although this is less than the requirement for amendments in the United States, it was rigid enough practically to exclude fundamental changes in the distribution of powers. That they could not muster a two-thirds majority for this purpose was not peculiar to the German people.

As to the first defect, i.e. proportional representation, its disadvantages were widely felt. Yet that was not enough. To change the electoral procedure for the Reichstag it was necessary to convince two-thirds of the elected members themselves that they were not the desirable type of delegates to represent the people. To get members of any legislature to admit their own inadequacy will always be a hard job. It was tried in 1924. Stopping short of an amendment to the Constitution, the reform bill introduced by the administration restricted itself to increasing the number of election districts to almost five times the old number, i.e. from 35 to 156, so that much smaller ones would replace the huge districts with their long lists of party candidates to be elected on straight party tickets. In the new districts the number of candidates that any group would be allowed to nominate was cut down to two. It was hoped that this change would assimilate election campaigns to those held under majority election systems and that it would have a wholesome influence on the type of candidates and also bring more youthful elements into the legislature. The cabinet and the Federal Council adopted the bill. The representatives in the Reichstag elected under the proportional system, however, could not be persuaded to vote themselves out of office. Their leaders, having nothing to fear for themselves, were willing to vote for the bill. Not so the rank and file. The bill was not even discussed. Another attempt, made in 1930, also failed.[3] This story should serve as a warning to future constitution makers.

Reform of the Federal Structure

A fourth grave shortcoming in the Weimar Constitution was its peculiar federal system. Prussia's government, ruling over three-fifths of the sixty-odd million Reich citizens and over two-thirds of the national area, was just another central government rather than a regional one. Formerly the monarch, being both Prussian king and German emperor at the same time, had kept the two governments in harmony, by his constitutional right to appoint the ministers in both without regard to parliamentary majorities. Now two parliaments with different majorities supported central cabinets of a different, and often of a contrasting, composition. In a kind of historical antithesis to the imperial period it was now the Prussian parliament which happened to be more democratically composed than was the federal. Consequently, as we have seen, it maintained cabinets composed of Social Democrats, Liberals, and Catholics, with Social Democratic Otto Braun as prime minister, almost without interruption throughout the entire republican period. National Liberals were added to the representatives of these three parties only from 1921 to 1925. German Nationals or other Conservatives never entered a Prussian cabinet during the democratic period. The Reich cabinet, on the other hand, had no Social Democratic

[3] The 1930 bill provided for 162 election districts, to be pooled in 31 combines and 12 regional groups for the transfer of surplus votes to other candidates of the same party. No ticket was to contain more than three names of candidates.

members from June 1920 to May 1921, from November 1922 to August 1923, from November 1923 to June 1928, and again from March 1930 to the end of the Republic. Instead, it included National Liberals from 1922 to 1932 without interruption and also German Nationals at several periods.

Braun was careful not to hamper the federal government too much in essential matters. He often showed the mettle of a veritable statesman by not using his powers when he might have done so in support of his own politics or those of his party. But there remained a good deal of friction. Much as regional and local autonomy was desirable from the democratic point of view, there was little justification for a second *central* government. The increasing administrative activities of the Reich led to duplications in centralized machinery and to conflicts in administrative practice.

In addition to this so-called 'Prussian Question' there were other shortcomings in the federal system. A number of small states were like patches on the map of Germany. They consisted in several instances of innumerable pieces of unconnected territory. The boundaries conflicted with economic requirements. The distribution of powers between the federal government and the states was not satisfactory, as was glaringly visible in their different policies in regard to law enforcement. Federal public works, federal unemployment insurance, federal assistance to workers who had exhausted their insurance benefits, and federal financial dealings brought the national administration into immediate contact with the municipalities and left the relation between federal, state, and local government in a precarious condition. The whole system needed overhauling.

The fight for reform in this matter was based not merely on theory or apprehensions but on practical experience. It was taken up by the national cabinet in 1928. In a joint meeting with the cabinets of the various states a commission was appointed, consisting of ten representatives of the Reich government and ten of the state governments, to prepare a change. At that time the chancellorship passed into the hands of a Social Democrat, Hermann Müller. Prussia's representative, joined by other members of the committee, offered the radical proposal that Prussia should disappear as a single separate government unit. The Prussian government and the Reich government should be merged in all matters that would still require centralized administration. Their regional and local agencies also should be merged, so that the so-called 'dualism' of the federal government and the Prussian government would be eliminated at all levels. The thirteen Prussian provinces, eventually to be rounded out into regions of a more reasonable shape, should become both regional districts for the federal agencies and simultaneously autonomous districts for home-rule affairs, although slightly different in their constitutional position from the remaining major *länder* (states) in the southern part of Germany. The smallest states would be fitted into these new autonomous units. Similar proposals were promoted from non-partisan movements in the country. The details were worked out in two sub-committees. Passionate debates on states' rights were overcome by the fortunate device of discussing the various administrative functions of government one by one. Thus it was in most cases easy to come to an agreement.

The final vote was taken at the beginning of Brüning's chancellorship, in June 1930. Having been a member of the commission before, he now presided over it. The report on the work of the two sub-committees—delivered by the Prussian member, who served on both—contained the following passages:

The proposals, as submitted to you by the majorities of the two sub-committees, imply complete elimination of the dualism between the Reich and Prussia both in central and provincial jurisdictions. For, all central and provincial authorities of the Reich and Prussian governments will be merged [on each level]. Henceforth, there is to be only one central government. The function of the present Reich agencies and Prussian state agencies are to be performed uniformly by Reich agencies, except in so far as they may be transferred to the home-rule authorities in provinces and communes.[4]

The proposals were passed by an overwhelming majority of 15 to 3 with two abstentions. The majority included the Chancellor, the representative of Prussia, and those of Saxony, Württemberg, and Baden.

One of the few questions that raised any difficulty was whether legislation in matters for which the southern states were to retain the right to legislate whereas the Prussian provinces were not separately to receive it—such as in matters of police and education—should be enacted for the Prussian sections by the whole Reichstag, or only by those members that were elected from the Prussian sections (*itio in partes*), or by a special legislature elected in these sections. This issue was recognized to be of secondary importance only, and its decision was left to the legislative bodies with the suggestion that the solution mentioned first, i.e. legislation by the entire Reichstag, should be the final aim, while the second or third solution, i.e. *itio in partes* or separate legislature, might be used during a transitional period.

The chances for a constitutional amendment were good. The need for reform was generally recognized, and minor points of disagreement were not likely to affect the final votes in the two houses, once the procedure was set going. Even the Bavarian representative, Prime Minister Heinrich Held, who voted against the majority in the commission, had no

[4] Translation as in A. Brecht, 'European Federation—The Democratic Alternative,' in *Harvard Law Review*, vol. 55 (1942), pp. 561, 570.

intention of obstructing the legitimate procedure of a constitutional amendment. He expressly recognized the need for a
strong federal power.

Brüning postponed taking up this matter while the urgent
problems of foreign and financial affairs absorbed the cabinet's working capacity to the limit. Yet he was prepared to
go ahead after the conclusion of the reparation negotiations
and the stabilization of the budget.

VII

'Fighting Fascism by Fighting Democracy'

Brüning Dismissed

AT THE END OF MAY—ONLY A FEW WEEKS BEFORE THE DATE set for the final conference on the reparation debt—Hindenburg suddenly dismissed Brüning and appointed Franz von Papen Chancellor. This surprising act made history.

Hindenburg's motives have never been completely explained. Differences of opinion on agrarian policy seem to have played a considerable part. According to a federal statute of 1931 financial aid could be given to farmers in the eastern parts of Germany for purposes of reorganization. It could, however, be made a condition for such aid that the owners surrender appropriate sections of their property for settlement by small farmers. Brüning was willing to insist on this latter condition, in agreement with the Prussian cabinet, to an extent which brought him into conflict with the great landowners. He was further inclined to favor an objective examination of each individual case, to determine whether the estate could be placed on a financially sound basis through the planned procedure, and if this proved impossible, to refuse financial aid. This was called Bolshevism by the landed aristocracy.

The aging President seemed to side with the landowners. Wire-pullers may have finally got hold of him in this matter as well as in others. His mind was becoming senile, so that he probably was no longer fully aware of what was going on around him. Brüning later told me that there were days when

Hindenburg did not even recognize him. The Chancellor often found the President influenced by others, but as a rule he was able to win him back. Otto Braun in his memoirs describes the impression he received when he saw Hindenburg in October of that year:

I had not seen the Reich President for a long time. At this conference [30 October], the last at which we ever met, Hindenburg made such an upsetting impression upon me of being senile [*einen erschütternd greisenshaften Eindruck*] that my indignation over his decree [of 20 July, removing the Prussian cabinet] was pushed into the background of my mind by a feeling of pity for this old man, who out of a sense of duty had once more assumed the burden of the presidential office and who was now being taken advantage of so infamously by unscrupulous men.[1]

It has furthermore been said that Hindenburg's acceptance of a valuable gift, the Neudeck estate in East Prussia, from great landowners and leading industrialists had made him more inclined to comply with their wishes and exposed him to the influence of his agrarian neighbors, whenever he spent vacations on his estate, as he did after the elections.

In addition, Hindenburg's conservative friends reproached him for disbanding only the Storm Troops while the republican *Reichsbanner* organization continued to exist. He was finally confronted with disturbing events in the ministry of defense. The democratic General Gröner, minister of defense, was also minister of the interior. In his latter capacity he had proposed and countersigned the decree against the Storm Troops. He explained its necessity to the Reichstag. His speeches brought him into conflict with his first aide in the defense ministry, General von Schleicher, who with other generals warned against combining the political position of

[1] Otto Braun, *Von Weimar zu Hitler*, Europa Verlag, New York, 1938, p. 417. See also the chapter on the agrarian policy in East Prussia, pp. 385-90.

minister of the interior with that of defense minister. Gröner resigned from his military post. Schleicher, whom Hindenburg wanted to appoint in Gröner's stead, was unwilling to assume office in the existing cabinet. This may have been a further reason for Hindenburg's decision in regard to Brüning. Last but not least, Hindenburg may have seriously hoped that a more conservative Chancellor would have a better chance of overcoming Fascism than Brüning had.

It is beyond the purpose of this investigation to examine the personal causes of the old man's sudden shift in policy. They are not really important for the world at large. There will always be human frailty, whether of old age, of vanity, insanity, or corruption. There will always be intrigues and wire-pulling around persons who wield great power. Predilections or views will always clash. Unique as each individual incarnation of these factors appears to the participants and historians, they are at bottom the most common features in the history of governments. They constitute the very reason why covenants and constitutions have been framed to provide effective checks against abuses of power. What matters now in retrospect is, therefore, whether such checks were provided by the German Constitution, how those that existed were used, and how events influenced the fight against Fascism in Germany.

In democratic and parliamentary terms, there was no justification for Brüning's dismissal from office. He had suffered no defeat in the Reichstag. On the contrary, a motion of censure against him had been defeated as late as the middle of May. Papen was not the recognized leader of the Opposition but a dark horse, a disaffected member of the Center Party in the Prussian Diet, without backing either there or in the national parliament. In the latter, he obviously commanded no more than a handful of votes. The change, then, was in flagrant disregard of parliamentary principles.

Unfortunately, it constituted no equally flagrant violation of the Weimar Constitution, which had established in a carelessly broad formulation the right of the President to appoint and dismiss the Chancellor.[2] The only limitation to this presidential right could be found in the clause stating that the Chancellor needed the confidence of the Reichstag. The Constitution did not even say that the Chancellor could not be dismissed so long as he had that confidence. It could furthermore be questioned whether Brüning actually had the confidence of the Reichstag. Although there was no majority willing to overthrow him, neither was there any to support him by a positive expression of confidence. If Hindenburg had replaced him with a man who was positively backed by a majority, no constitutional objection could have been raised. There was in fact not the slightest indication of a majority willing to back Papen. But again, it could be argued that it was the technical right of the President to find out whether a new Chancellor could obtain a majority backing and that even new elections could be held for that purpose. The wording of the Constitution lent itself to such interpretation. In addition, Brüning was dismissed only after he had handed in the cabinet's resignation. He had done so when the President had notified him that he was no longer willing to give him his confidence or to sign the decrees the Chancellor wanted to submit to him. Having neither a positive majority in the Reichstag to enact the laws he proposed, nor the assurance that the President would sign them as emergency decrees, he tendered his resignation. This was on the 30th of May, and the dismissal was signed on the 1st of June.

The letter of the Constitution, therefore, was not violated. As to its living spirit, there was no precedent in the history of the young Republic to meet the situation. It was the first

[2] See Appendix D.

time that Hindenburg used his broad powers in this way. Hence it was also the first occasion for the Reichstag—or rather for the people, since the Reichstag was being dissolved over the countersignature of the new Chancellor—to establish a precedent *against* Hindenburg's interpretation of the Constitution by the manner in which they responded to the challenge in the forthcoming elections. Such had been the historical answer given fifty-five years earlier in a French election, when, also in the month of May, another popular general as President used a similar ambiguity in the French fundamental laws in a similar way. President MacMahon, on 16 May 1877 dismissed the republican prime minister, Jules Simon, who had been supported by a majority, and appointed a monarchist, the Duc de Broglie, giving him authority to dissolve the chamber. The result was that, in response to Gambetta's popular leadership in the election campaign, the two-thirds republican majority which only recently had replaced the former majority for monarchic restoration, was re-elected in spite of all governmental machinations.

The German people in 1932, while clearly repudiating Papen, did not respond so positively in favor of parliamentary democracy. Instead, they split into three or four main blocks favoring three or four mutually incompatible types of government—communism, fascism, democracy, and constitutional monarchy—symbolized by hostile flags: the red flag of the Communists with sickle and hammer, the swastika flag of the National Socialists, the black-red-gold flag of the Republic, and the black-white-red flag of the Monarchy.[3] None of these main blocks obtained a majority, nor did even the democrats and constitutional monarchists together, as we shall see below. But much happened within the two months that passed between dissolution and elections and to that we must turn first.

[3] See also Appendix B.

Hindenburg and Papen, Too, Fight Totalitarianism

Regarding the fight against Fascism and Totalitarianism, the following is of the greatest importance for the historian.

When Hindenburg appointed Papen, the intention of neither was to surrender to totalitarian doctrines and to allow the National Socialists to apply their ideas of one-party rule. Strange as it may sound today, there is no doubt that at that time Hindenburg and Papen, too, intended to fight National Socialism. What they planned can best be described by saying that they wanted to overcome the National Socialists by taking the wind out of their sails and to steer a more conservative course. They were prepared to acknowledge the strength of Hitler's party by offering it seats in a coalition cabinet and thus giving it a share of power and responsibility, but only on condition that the party abandoned its absolute and totalitarian demands. How strictly they were opposed to these demands is proved by two official communiqués with regard to negotiations that took place between Hindenburg and Hitler. They were issued by the President's office as late as 13 August and 24 November 1932.

On 13 August Hitler had rejected Hindenburg's offer to enter Papen's cabinet as Vice Chancellor. Hitler demanded that the President should confer on himself 'the lead in the Reich Government and the entire state power [*die gesamte Staatsgewalt*] to its full extent.' Reporting on this request, the communiqué continued:

Reich President Hindenburg rejected this demand most definitely, giving as his reason that he could not bear the responsibility before his conscience and his duties towards the fatherland, if he conferred the entire power of government exclusively on the National Socialist movement which wanted to use this power one-sidedly.

After the November elections the Reich President again conferred with Hitler on the formation of a cabinet. Hitler made proposals which, on 24 November, the President rejected. His reasons were thus stated in the official communiqué:

The Reich President has rejected this proposal, because he feels that he cannot assume responsibility before the German people for granting his presidential full powers to the leader of a party that, time and again, has emphasized its exclusiveness, and because he must fear that a cabinet leaning on presidential powers [Präsidialkabinet], if led by Hitler, will inevitably develop into a party dictatorship with all its consequences of dreadful aggravation of antagonisms [Gegensätze] among the German people. The President cannot bear the responsibility under his oath and before his conscience for causing such aggravation.

The oath to which the President referred was the oath of loyalty to the Weimar Constitution.

Methods and Effects

Thus one might correctly speak of a political fight against Totalitarianism conducted by Hindenburg and Papen in those latter days of the German Republic. Yet their weapons were of a most ambiguous character. Extreme mildness towards the National Socialists on the one hand, even to an avowed agreement with them over their toleration of Papen's cabinet, and on the other, a frontal attack on the political Left—these were considered proper means by which to get the better of Hitler in popular esteem and in new elections.

After dissolving the Reichstag, the President over Papen's signature repealed the ban against private uniforms and revoked the decree dissolving the National Socialist Storm Troops, which he had issued only two months before. The Storm Troops could resume their parades in full panoply. The Prussian police who, directed by the Social Democratic Prussian minister of the interior, Carl Severing, had been busy for two months keeping Storm Troopers from the streets, had now to march along with them to protect them in their re-gained 'right of demonstration' from the attacks of the em-bittered Communists, whose Red-Front organization was still banned. The same day, 14 June, most other decrees of Brü-ning's regime that had been designed to protect public safety were also repealed. A supplementary decree of 28 June en-joined the state governments from issuing protective meas-ures similar to those of Brüning.

The immediate effect of this radical change in policy was that bloody fights flared up more fiercely than ever. In the second half of June, according to figures issued by the Papen administration, 17 were killed, 5 Communists and 12 National Socialists, many more than in any previous month. In July, 86 died a violent death, 30 Communists, 38 National Social-ists, and 18 others. These figures of fatal casualties can, how-ever, hardly convey an adequate idea of the violence in great parts of the Reich that took place day by day. Let us add brief notes for a few calendar days in early August:

1 August: Attempts in Königsberg on the Prussian district president, and on a city councillor, who died from his wounds. Two Communists and two leaders of the Social Democratic Party seriously wounded. Bombs thrown at three newspaper buildings.

2 August: Bombs planted in ten towns in Holstein Prov-ince, pistol shots fired in Marienburg and hand grenades thrown at the People's House in Liegnitz and at the county office in Goldberg.

3 August: the Mayor of Norgau shot dead. Bomb plot against the synagogue in Kiel. A National Socialist killed in Kreuzburg.

4 August: Two police officers killed in Gleiwitz. Incendi-

ary bombs thrown at a department store in Ortelsburg, and at a land-title office in the county of Labiau.

5 August: Bomb plot against the Reichsbank branch office in Lötzen.

6 August: Hand grenades directed against a pharmacy in Lyck, pistol shots at a Communist home in Tilsit, hand grenades used in Breslau, Gleiwitz and Ratibor, bombs and pistol shots in Kiel, a dynamiting attempt in Braunschweig.

7 August: Leader of the republican *Reichsbanner* organization shot to death in Lötzen, hand grenades thrown at a Catholic newspaper office and a municipal health insurance office in Ratibor, twelve other attempts in Silesia alone.

9 August: More than twenty attempts with grenades, bombs and pistols in Silesia and East Prussia, causing the death of two persons in Silesia. Attempt on a newspaper building in Stettin. A Reichsbanner member found dead in the county of Leobschütz. A National Socialist torn to pieces by his own hand grenade in Reichenbach, Silesia. On the same day, in the Silesian village of Potempa, a Communist, called Pietzruch, brutally murdered in the presence of his mother by five National Socialists.[4]

Papen's government was soon forced to re-issue most of the decrees it had repealed and, on 9 August, even to order the death penalty for clashes that resulted in persons being killed. Although the Storm Troops were not being disbanded, parades and public meetings in the open air were generally prohibited and thus the Brown Shirts were kept from part at least of their activities.

[4] The foregoing material is taken from *Preussen contra Reich vor dem Staatsgerichtshof* (J. H. W. Dietz, Berlin, 1933), with an introduction by Arnold Brecht, pp. 16 ff.

Dismissal of the Prussian State Ministers

In the midst of these bloody clashes, on 20 July, only eleven days before the elections, a new event stirred the people. Hindenburg by presidential decree based on Article 48 of the Weimar Constitution appointed Papen over the latter's countersignature Commissioner for Prussia.[5] Papen, under the broad authority delegated to him, dismissed the eight ministers of the Prussian parliamentary cabinet, and he and his deputies took over their posts. The Prussian prime minister was still the Social Democrat Otto Braun, who had held that office almost uninterruptedly since 1920. The minister of the interior and chief of the Prussian police was Carl Severing, another Social Democrat of long standing. In addition, there were three Catholics, two Liberals, and a third Social Democrat in the cabinet. All were dismissed. They appealed to the Supreme Court for Constitutional Conflicts (*Staatsgerichtshof*), which the Constitution had provided should decide on conflicts between the national government, the state governments, and other political bodies. They acknowledged that Article 48 granted the President the power for purposes that were in line with the Constitution to take over the state and local police and many other functions of state government, but they protested that the outright dismissal of parliamentary state ministers by federal decree was unconstitutional.

It certainly was unconstitutional, and the Supreme Court, in its decision of 25 October, stated so. However far reaching the authority granted the Reich President in Article 48, the Court pronounced that he could not dismiss state ministers, he could not alter or impair their relation to their state assemblies, he could not crowd them or their delegates out of the federal second chamber, the Reichsrat, and he could not disallow them the use of their constitutional right—a

[5] See Appendix E.

peculiarity of the German Constitution—of addressing the Reichstag in their capacity as representatives of their state. And another important point was also decided by the Supreme Court Judges. They said they could leave it an open question whether Article 48 gave broader powers to the President in case a state government had violated its constitutional duties towards the Reich government. For, so the Court stated as a result of the long hearing, in no case *had* the state of Prussia violated its constitutional duties towards the federal government.

Error, Guilt, or Reasonable Choice?

Since it was so obvious that Hindenburg and Papen had violated the Constitution on 20 July 1932, why did the Prussian ministers appeal only to the Court? Why did they not call on the masses for an open fight, as the Social Democratic members of the government had done on 13 March 1920, on the night of the Kapp Putsch? Were they wavering in their defense of democratic principles? Had they lost their faith in democracy? Did they not feel the historic responsibility of the hour? Or were they simply cowards? Most critics seem to agree that the Prussian government should have called on the masses at that time. While there were few flagrant violations of the Constitution on any particular later date, up to the dissolution of parties in July 1933, because of the legalistic disguise used by Hitler's autocratic regime, there was a clear breach of the Constitution on 20 July 1932. The question, therefore, at what time the workers should have rebelled, is now most generally answered, 'On the 20th of July 1932.' Few, however, have cared to reconstruct the situation as it was then.

It was a triangular fight. The democratic parties fought Papen. But, first of all, they fought Hitler. Papen, first of all, fought the Communists and the Social Democrats. Yet he still fought Hitler's ambition to obtain unlimited power. In

abstaining from street fights against Hindenburg and Papen
and using only the constitutional remedy of an appeal to the
court, the Prussian ministers were led by the desire to preserve the constitutional basis of governmental powers and to
force Hindenburg back within constitutional bounds. Only
four months had passed since they had publicly confessed
their belief in the righteous intentions and the good faith of
the President. Should they now call for civil war against him
without first using the constitutional remedies? All arms were
on the other side. It has often been asserted that the Prussian
police were completely in the hands of Severing and would
have protected the Prussian ministers if called upon. This is
a grave mistake. There was no doubt but that the President
had by Article 48 authority to take over Prussia's entire police
force. Ebert had done so several times. The Prussian police
officers, although faithful to their duties and loyally attached
to Severing, knew that this was so. Therefore, in the event
of an appeal to violent resistance, the Reich President would
have been supported by the Army, by the 'Steel Helmet'
organization of former soldiers and of Conservatives, by the
Storm Troops of the Nazis, and also by the civil servants
and the police. Neither the police nor other civil servants,
with a very few exceptions, would have fought against the
legitimate President who had the constitutional authority to
call them up.

All this was in striking contrast to the situation in 1920,
when the Reich President himself led the fight against the
violators of the Constitution and was supported by the Civil
Service and at least by parts of the Army and police, in addition to the workers. In 1932, the Prussian ministers could
have relied only on unarmed workers, and not even on all
of them. They foresaw that a call to active resistance would
result in the immediate end of the Republic, and in a mas-
sacre of the defenseless workers. They felt that they could

not assume responsibility for such a certain end, as long as there was any alternative that promised better results for the democratic Republic. And such an alternative there seemed to be. There was hope that moderation, and the appeal to the Supreme Court, would manœuvre Papen into a critical situation, and the National Socialists with him. In this hope they were not deceived.

Three further points made the fighting strength of the Prussian ministers particularly weak at that time. They had been given a vote of no-confidence in their parliament three months before and kept office only pending negotiations for the formation of a new cabinet. Secondly, most of them—and most of their adherents—were not interested in the preservation of the existing state of Prussia. They agreed in principle that the Reich and Prussian governments should be merged, but they wanted to see this result achieved by constitutional methods. Thirdly, the cabinet consisted not only of Social Democrats and militant Liberals, but also of Catholics, who would not have gone beyond an appeal to the Court. But these were minor points as compared with the basic considerations.

From July to December 1932

The appeal to the Supreme Court did force Hindenburg and Papen to be most careful in their proceedings pending the decision of the Court. Almost day by day they tried to demonstrate that they were abiding by the Constitution. The failure of their 'take-the-wind-out-of-the-sail' policy was at once revealed by the elections held on 31 July. The new Reichstag was less capable of forming a majority cabinet than any of its predecessors. It consisted of 230 National Socialists, more than double the former number, and 89 Communists, together making 319, leaving a minority of only 288 seats to all other parties, including those of the democrats as well as the monarchists. Even if all of them had supported a cabinet, it would have been overthrown by the negative majority of National Socialists and Communists. The Communists, at that time, were stubbornly clinging to their policy of supporting any vote of no-confidence even with their deadly fascist enemies. Nor were several of the bourgeois parties willing to form a cabinet against the Right with the support of the Communists. No democratic genius could have produced a democratic government out of such a parliament.

Compared with 1928 the National Socialists had gained almost thirteen million votes. Six million obviously came from the Rightist parties who, including the National Liberals, lost that many. The remaining seven million seem to have come mainly from new voters, who numbered six million.[6] The two Catholic parties had together a gain of more than one parties, taken together, a gain of almost one million. These million votes over their number in 1928, and the two Labor parties cannot, therefore, have contributed much towards the National Socialist victory. One or two million may have gone over to the National Socialists from those who in 1928 voted for democratic candidates, yet the main role in the swing to the National Socialists must have been played by young voters, especially those without jobs; by former non-voters, stirred by propaganda and recent events; and by members of the Rightist parties.

The overwhelming majority of the new Reichstag was definitely opposed to Papen. In this respect the Reichstag was all but unanimous. No positive platform, however, could possibly be formed by the four antagonistic blocs of communists, democrats, monarchists, and fascists. Not even the monarchists and fascists combined, or the democrats and

[6] See the excellent analysis by Sidney L. W. Mellon, 'The German People and the Postwar World,' *American Political Science Review*, vol. 37 (1943), pp. 601, 621.

monarchists combined, could form a majority. Unless the Catholic Center and the National Socialists came to some practical understanding, there was no majority conceivable to back a cabinet. When feelers were put out by some of the Catholics to the National Socialists or vice versa, no one was now more bitterly opposed to such a combination than Papen. He went so far as to publish an article under his name in which he warned against party tactics and manœuvres designed to oust him. And he asked the question, withholding his own answer for the time being, who would be the deceiver and who would be the dupe in such a coalition, which at any rate would be at the cost of the German people.[7]

The Reichstag was dissolved once more. The methods the Chancellor used to forestall by repeated dissolution any steps the new Reichstag might take against him or his decrees brought him into new conflicts. The tension between Papen and the National Socialists came into the open before the dissolution by a row between him and Hermann Göring, then President of the Reichstag. A vote, the validity of which was controversial, showed a majority of 510 against the Chancellor and only 42 for him, with 5 abstaining.

Pending the elections, Papen now saw himself compelled to proceed against the National Socialists more and more rigidly. He had to go beyond his general ban of meetings in the open air by forbidding a mass meeting of National Socialists, planned to be held indoors in the Berlin Sport Palace, where Dr. Goebbels was scheduled to speak. Similar orders were issued prohibiting indoor meetings of National Socialists in the Rhineland, East Prussia, and elsewhere. The reasons given for these police measures, couched in more general terms than those used by Severing in similar orders, were

[7] Franz von Papen, 'Konservative Staatsführung,' in *Deutsche Allgemeine Zeitung*, 1 September 1932, evening ed. (No. 410). He did not seem to remember this article four months later, when he made his pact with Hitler.

that the National Socialists had constantly disturbed meetings of other groups and that there was danger, therefore, that in public meetings held by National Socialists mere interruptions by their opponents would be suppressed with violence. National Socialist newspapers, too, were forbidden in the Rhineland for some time.[8]

The hearings before the Supreme Court in the case of Prussia *vs.* Reich took place between 10 and 17 October, i.e. only a few weeks before the new elections, which were held on 6 November. The great publicity given the court proceedings in the domestic press went far towards undermining both Papen's and Hitler's power. The precise analysis of the political events as given during the hearings of the case, and the final decision, which was rendered by the Chief Justice in open court on 25 October immediately before the elections,[9] had a decisive influence on the election results.

It was the first great set-back for the National Socialists. They lost two million votes and 34 seats. Their percentage of the votes sank slightly below one-third. Many were downhearted. Goebbels noted in his diary on election day: 'Each new report brings new defeat.' The following day, he wrote: 'There is a great deal of despair among the voters.' On 11 November: 'I receive a report on the financial situation of the Berlin organization. That situation is quite desperate. Nothing but low tide, debts, and commitments, and in addition the complete impossibility after this defeat of getting money in adequate amounts anywhere.' On 6 December: 'The situation is catastrophic. In Thuringia we have suffered a loss of almost 40 per cent since 31 July.' On 8 December: 'The organization is dominated by deep depression. Financial worries make all constructive work impossible . . . We are all deeply de-

[8] See *Preussen contra Reich vor dem Staatsgerichtshof* (as cited Chapter VII), pp. 395-6.
[9] See Appendix E.

pressed, especially because there is now the danger that the entire party will disintegrate and that all our work has been for nothing.' And on 15 December: 'It is high time that we should get into power. There is, it is true, not the slightest chance at the time being.' [10]

Had then the Prussian democrats been so wrong in appealing to the Court rather than to the unarmed fists of the workers, who would have had the entire armed forces of Germany against them? And it was not only the Nazis that had suffered defeat. Papen, too, was so deeply discredited by his defeat in the Prussian trial and in the elections that Hindenburg had to discard him. On 2 December, the President appointed General von Schleicher, after rejecting Hitler's claims to the chancellorship in the statement of 24 November, as quoted above. Whatever Schleicher's character and share in the intrigues may have been, there is no doubt that he was determined to avert outright Fascism and Totalitarianism. He was willing to come to an agreement with the Trade Unions, with the Prussian government, and with the moderate wing of the National Socialists under Gregor Strasser, but not with Hitler.

[10] *Vom Kaiserhof zur Reichskanzlei*, Eher, Munich, 1934, pp. 196 ff.

VIII

Hitler's Oath

Hitler Paralyzes His Opponents by Swearing Allegiance to Their Constitution

THEN ANOTHER EVENT OCCURRED THAT UPSET ALL CALCULA-tions and one that no one had foreseen. Papen, disgruntled by his failure, joined forces with Hitler. He prevailed on Hindenburg to dismiss Schleicher abruptly and to appoint Hitler as Chancellor and himself as Vice Chancellor. His main argument seems to have been that Schleicher could not obtain a majority in the Reichstag, that he conspired against Hindenburg, and that therefore there was no way out except to appoint Hitler. Hitler, so Papen argued, was after all still the leader of the biggest party, he was now ready to accept a coalition cabinet, and such coalition between National Socialists and German Nationals, although not yet commanding a majority, might obtain one after new elections. On the very date that had been set for the final arrangement between Schleicher and the Prussian ministers, Schleicher was dismissed and subsequently Hitler was appointed Chancellor of the German Reich.

Hitler, then, did not assume power as a usurper, as Kapp had done in 1920. He was called into office as the leader of the party that held the greatest number of seats in the legislature. He was appointed by the legitimate President of the Republic, who had the constitutional power to appoint anyone whom he thought able to obtain the necessary support in the Reichstag, and certainly, to try out the leader of the largest group. Hitler entered office as the head of a coalition cabinet, in which the majority of positions was left to Conservatives and former civil servants. He took the oath of allegiance to the Weimar Constitution, as he had already done a short time before, when his appointment to a Brunswick minor office made him, the former Austrian, a German citizen.[1] He now took, as Chancellor, the oath as formulated in Section 3 of the *Reichsministergesetz* of 27 March 1930:

I shall work with all my might for the welfare of the German People. I shall abide by [*wahren*, which in German includes the meaning of guard and preserve] the Constitution and the laws of the German People; conscientiously fulfil the duties incumbent upon me; and conduct my office impartially and with justice towards everybody [*unparteiisch und gerecht gegen jedermann*].

Thus Hitler was now the *legitimate* Chancellor, according to the formalistic interpretation of the Constitution that had so often been applied before, and the civil servants, courts, and foreign diplomats would certainly acknowledge him as such. Legitimate, at least, until he should flagrantly violate the letter of the Constitution, or until the legislature should pass a vote of censure against him and back a new candidate. The President dissolved the legislature, as he had done before, to see whether the people endorsed the appointment. There was no indication that the Reichstag would be sent home for good. On the contrary, new elections were set for the nearest date that was technically possible, the 5th of March.

No one, least of all his own followers, believed that Hitler *would* preserve the Weimar Constitution. But to rise against him the first night would make the rebels the technical violators of the Constitution that they wanted to defend. All the armed forces of the Reich, the fascist Storm Troops, the

[1] See Appendix C.

conservative Steel Helmet troops, the police, and the rigidly legalistic civil servants would clamp down upon them and brand them as traitors to their own Constitution. They had to wait; wait for the first grave violation of the Constitution by Hitler. In the meantime they had to prevent an election success of the new coalition. They rushed to their campaign activities.

If the first stage of their political fight against Fascism had ended in failure, through Hitler's appointment, this was due to a preposterous concatenation of adverse circumstances. No one can justly say that it was because of the absence of any fight. And another fight, harder than the old one, lay ahead.

IX

A Period of Suspense

Legality?

LOOKING BACK WITH THE KNOWLEDGE THAT WE NOW HAVE of subsequent events, one might assume that no serious doubt could have prevailed what the consequences would be of Hitler's appointment. However, when people were looking forward at that early date, the vast majority were far from anticipating the real outcome. Grave apprehensions, indeed, there were, and in some instances forecasts were to prove highly accurate. Yet there is a great difference between mere apprehensions and established facts. Apprehensions may be wrong. Only independent minds of unusual capacity are able to take their misgivings for more than a nightmare and to draw realistic conclusions, as long as the normal pattern of life and the usual aspect of one's surroundings have not substantially changed. Those who had such clear vision found it impossible to convince people at large.

Too many factors could be enumerated that might prevent dismal anticipations of a reign of terror and oppression, of arbitrary despotism and wholesale persecutions, of war and humiliation, from becoming true. First, Hitler was not vested with absolute power. The power given him was only that of a Chancellor under the Weimar Constitution. Secondly, the majority in his cabinet were not National Socialists, but Conservatives—Catholics, like Papen; Protestants, like Hugenberg and Seldte; or civil servants, like Constantin von Neurath in the foreign office, and Count Lutz Schwerin von Krosigk in the ministry of finance. They would do their best to avert terroristic methods and arbitrary despotism. Thirdly, there was Hindenburg, whose power under the Constitution had proved superior to that of the Chancellor during the last two years. Fourthly, there were the independent courts, the civil servants, and there was the Army, certainly authoritarian and militaristic in its general outlook, but animated by traditional concepts very different from those of National Socialism, and jealously hostile to granting the Storm Troopers of the party any appearance of superiority. Fifthly, there were the foreign countries, which in their own interest would see to it that no despotic and militaristic regime should take the place of a constitutional government. After all, there was some hope left.

Pious Proclamation by the Cabinet

The first proclamation of the new cabinet, of 1 February, seemed to support such an optimistic outlook. Although very outspoken in its goal that Communism should be destroyed in Germany, and while not free from threats towards Social Democrats in case they should support Communism, it otherwise avoided threatening anyone. The Jews, on whom a violent attack had been feared during the first nights because of preceding Nazi propaganda, were not even mentioned. Positively, the document stated that the cabinet wanted to solve the economic crisis by two great four-year plans, the one designed to save the farmer, the other to overcome unemployment. After four years, both aims would be reached. 'Well, German People, give us four years' time, and then judge and pass sentence on us.' Once more, legality was referred to. 'Faithful to our oath,' the cabinet said, it turned to the German people for election, thus implying that it did not seek extra-constitutional powers. It appealed for 'conciliation,' except only with the Communists. The question of rearmament was adumbrated in a negative way. 'Great as our love of our Army is, we would yet be delighted [*beglückt*, a rare and strong expression in German speech] if the world by restricting their armaments made an increase in our own weapons for ever unnecessary.' The value of tradition was praised, and the religious basis of the moral standards of government stressed at several places. 'May Almighty God,' thus the proclamation ended, 'take our work under His mercy, shape our will the right way, bless our understanding, and make us happy with the confidence of our nation.' No democratic statement of policy had ever employed such pious language. Eleven signatures of the members of the cabinet demonstrated visibly that only three were National Socialists, while eight were not.

How Far Will Hitler Go?

Nor was it quite certain whether Hitler himself was actually poised to go the fascist way to the limit. He had sworn several times that he would keep within the boundaries of law. His personality was an altogether unfamiliar type to Germans as well as to the world abroad. There were strange contradictions in his very appearance. Alternately, he seemed plain and resourceful, soldierlike and mystical, intelligent and foolish, disciplined and hysterical. When he spoke to a large audience, his voice was harsh and his threats sounded barbaric. Yet in a small private circle his speech could be soft and well modulated, and his eyes could appear friendly and frank. Observers who believed they were able to understand the inner functioning of such public figures as Papen or Schleicher, Brüning or Ebert, Bismarck or Napoleon, and even Lenin or Mussolini, were at a loss when they stared at Hitler's face that looked completely empty to them. Once he had attained power, he might have the ambition to become a great and constructive statesman, accessible to reasonable advice. 'In the long run,' one of the co-operating ministers said to the present writer, 'the world is always ruled by reason.' It was reassuring to think in such terms for those who did not realize what 'in the long run' might mean.

As to the party, two or more wings were easily distinguishable. There were the extreme Nazis, who were looking out for adventure, vengeance, and brutality. Yet there were also those who, although intent on the realization of some fundamental ideas, seemed otherwise amenable and serious in their arguments. Much would depend on whether Hitler would act under the pressure of the extremists in his party or use the great official power he now possessed to do away with that wing of his followers. Everyone else would wish him well if he tried to do so.

The Federal Council

As if eager to abide by old custom, Hitler presented himself to the Federal Council (Reichsrat) the very next day after the proclamation, i.e. on 2 February. His address was moderate and differed little from other speeches that had often been made on like occasions from the same chair. It was answered, on behalf of the Council, by the representative of the largest state, Prussia, reinstated in his seat by the Supreme Court a few weeks before. Starting from Hitler's various references to tradition and legality, the speaker said:

Mr. Chancellor—In accordance with an old custom it devolves upon me to reply for the Federal Council to your address.

The room in which we are meeting is the same room, unchanged, that was used by the old [imperial] Bundesrat. The order in which the various states are seated is much as it was in Bismarck's time; Prussia at the Chancellor's right, Bavaria at his left, followed by the other states, the number recently enriched by the presence in our midst, at the other side of the table, of the representatives elected from the Prussian provinces. Likewise, the procedure in plenary sessions and in committee meetings has remained as it used to be. Even today, there are still some of those among us who sat here prior to the [First World] War. Only slowly have their ranks been thinned, not all at once after the war.

Tradition, then, is at home in this room to a high degree, and a specifically German tradition at that. This holds true also for the spirit of the deliberations and for the personal relations between the members of the Federal Council and the Reich Cabinet. Within the Council objectivity, temperate argument in controversies, and the cultivation of friendly and comradelike relations have been the custom, no exception to which has come to our knowledge.

This atmosphere, which very rarely breaks into thunderstorms, is necessary for the performance of the Council's organic function which, if not in the strictly legal sense, is actually that of a first or, to put it more modestly, a second chamber. The Federal Council is the balance within the German clockwork, not its motor or spring. It is its duty to see to it that every matter is dealt with in a strictly objective way [*streng sachlich*, i.e. without personal bias or 'politics']. It was meant to function, as it were, like the government's conscience in restless and passionate times. By no means a brake on energetic progress, but a brake on explosive passions and overheated controversies, and a support in all work conducted in a spirit of objectivity [*sachlicher Arbeit*], especially a support to the Federal Government in such work.

The experience and opinions of the German states and regions rally here. We are asking you, Mr. Chancellor, to be conscious of this institution's high value and to use it as is required by the Constitution and the Council's functions. According to the Constitution the Council is called upon to co-operate, not only in questions of legislation, but also of administration: it is to be kept informed on the conduct of federal affairs, and its committees are to be consulted by the federal Ministries in all important matters.

Then the speaker turning more directly to Hitler went on:

At present the Council's work is sensibly impaired by a peculiar situation. The Federal Government's proceeding in Prussia has affected not alone its relations to Prussia, but also those with the other states. The Council desires that this abnormal situation be cleared up as quickly as possible *in a constitutional way*.

You, Mr. Chancellor, have taken the grave step from your position as leader in a movement that has grown up in rigid opposition, to that of the *responsible* official who directs German policy [*verantwortlicher Leiter der deutschen Politik*]. This we feel has been a most serious decision for you personally, too. For it means that you have taken the grave duty upon yourself, and confirmed it by a solemn oath, to give your strength to the welfare of the *entire* people, to *abide by the Constitution* and the law of the land, conscientiously to fulfil the duties that devolve upon you, and to *conduct your office 'impartially, and with justice towards everybody.'* The entire Federal Council, strongly and with understanding, will always support you *in the fulfilment of these duties*.

The Cabinet is confronted with extremely difficult problems, especially the elimination of the depressing unemployment, which we know exists not in Germany alone but also in the United States and England, that is in countries of a completely different political situation. Agreeing with the Cabinet on the priority of this urgent question, the Council requests that you, Mr. Chancellor, co-operate closely with it in its solution. We appreciate that you have taken this early opportunity to present yourself to the Council.

Although couched in measured language in view of the ceremonious occasion and of the fact that the speaker was expected to express the opinion of the whole body rather than individual views, this exhortation with its literal repetition of Hitler's oath was unequivocal. It proved to be the last free speech delivered in the Council. Hitler rose hesitatingly, bowed stiffly to the Council, shook hands briefly with the speaker, and walked out without replying. The chancellery advised the speaker on the same evening that the Fuehrer was raging and that the four or five party members that had accompanied him to the meeting were even more furious. The National Socialist press, the following morning, spoke of an unheard-of challenge. Yet what Hitler's actual intentions were and how far he would respect the Constitution remained a matter of guesswork.

X

First Constitutional Conflict

'Legality Above, Revolution Below'

IN CONVERSATIONS WITH THE MEMBERS OF HIS CABINET AND
official advisers, Hitler used a most adroit formula in describ-
ing his own position. He was perfectly willing, he would say,
to govern in a legal way. Yet there was a national revolution
going on from below. This movement was a fact that he had
to take into account. He had to meet it in the proper way.
He was unable just to call it off. It *could* not be called off,
not even by him. He had to proceed very carefully in order
to prevent the worst. He could not strike with the usual
techniques of prosecution at every violation of law by his
partisans. It just would not work that way and if it should
be tried it could not but lead to terrible excesses. Instead, he
would have to show by determined action that a new period
of government had begun. He could then hope gradually to
succeed in directing the now turbulent forces of the National
Uprising into channels of the new order.

One of the deepest reasons for the revolt of his partisans,
he would add, was the leniency shown the Communists. The
people as a whole wanted to get rid of Communism as a
tolerated movement in Germany. This was absolutely necessary for the re-establishment of peace and order. Such had
also been the keynote of the cabinet's official proclamation.
'If Germany is to live and see this political and economic
recovery,' so it read, 'and if she is conscientiously to fulfil her
obligations towards the other nations, one decisive act is

required: to overcome the disintegration of Germany by Communism.'

The Supreme Court on Communism, on National Socialism, and on Hitler

These threats against Communism, strong as they were, could be viewed as part of a political program that was compatible with the law and the Constitution. The Supreme Court had frequently enunciated that the Communist Party was illegal in its aims, that it was preparing for the overthrow of constitutional government by violence, and that its plans were sufficiently substantiated to justify outlawing the party whenever the government should choose to do so. The police ministers in several states, especially the Social Democratic Prussian minister, Carl Severing, had often emphasized the illegality of the methods used by the Communists and had provided the Supreme Court with the evidence. It is true, both Severing and the Court had reached the same conclusion regarding the National Socialist Party. Differing from Severing in this respect, however, the Supreme Court had left it an open question whether Hitler himself approved of the illegal methods. 'It is indeed correct,' the opinion of the Supreme Court of 10 February 1931 read,

that the leader of the National Socialist Party [in the procedure against three Reichswehr officers in Ulm, September 1930] made a sworn statement that he was pursuing his goals only on strictly legal roads now. It is however notorious that the National Socialist Party aims at a change in the Reich Constitution and it follows from numerous articles of the National Socialist press that at least sections of the party are convinced that the change in the Constitution at which the party aims can only be effected by the use of violence, and for that the masses must be prepared ideologically. Therefore, even though Hitler may insist that revolutionary aims within the National Socialist Party must be suppressed and eventually punished with exclusion from the party, this does not preclude the possibility that such revolutionary aims are being pursued within the party without the approval of its leader Hitler and even against his will . . .

It was very much in line with these decisions of the Supreme Court that Hitler seemed to take his course at first. At any rate, in outlawing the Communist organizations the cabinet could refer to the jurisdiction of the Supreme Court.

The cabinet did not even go thus far immediately. The Communists were allowed to nominate their candidates for the elections of 5 March, and the party and their candidates received the place on the government-printed ballots as prescribed by law for legitimate parties. But Communist meetings were banned during the last two weeks of the campaign. Acts of violence committed against Communists fell under the heading of revolutionary acts from below that could not be helped.

'Red' Prussia's Cabinet Again Dismissed

The first constitutional conflict arose on an issue not touching the police and individual rights. The opinion of the Supreme Court *in re* Prussia had left the Reich cabinet in the possession of the Prussian police by virtue of the presidential emergency powers, and Hitler hastened to appoint Hermann Göring commissioner for police. The police therefore were firmly in party hands.

Yet Prussia's representation in the Federal Council and the Prussian legislature still were beyond Hitler's control. And the cabinet of Prussia was still democratic, or what National Socialists and German Nationals liked to call 'red,' because it contained Social Democrats. Prussia's Diet had obstinately refused to elect a National Socialist prime minister. Hitler therefore insisted that it should be dissolved and new elections

held on the same day as those for the Reichstag. Yet neither
the Reich President nor the Chancellor was constitutionally
entitled to dissolve the Prussian Diet. That could be done,
according to the Prussian Constitution, only by a three-man
board, composed of the prime minister, i.e. the Social Democrat Otto Braun; the president of the upper chamber, at that
time Conrad Adenauer, Catholic mayor of Cologne; and the
Diet's own president, National Socialist Hanns Kerrl. Otto
Braun had just been reinstated by the Supreme Court and expressly assured by the Court of the inviolability of his rights
in relation to the Diet. He and Adenauer were opposed to
dissolution, because they had no confidence that an election
campaign could be carried on in any spirit of fairness. They
were instead convinced that terror would be used against all
enemies of the Nazis. No emissaries from Hitler or Hindenburg could prevail on them to change their view.

This controversy led Hitler into his first conflict with
legality. On 6 February he elicited a presidential decree by
which the Prussian ministers were removed from all their
remaining functions and the vote of the prime minister on
the three-man board was transferred to the Reich Commissioner for Prussia, Franz von Papen. The latter was also to
represent Prussia in the Federal Council. To justify this decree in view of the October decision of the Supreme Court,
the Reich cabinet contended that *after* that decision the Prussian ministers had failed to perform their duty towards the
Reich, especially when they refused to dissolve the Prussian
Diet in a situation that required elections for a new Diet, since
it had been unable for almost a year to agree on a new cabinet. This alleged justification took advantage of a sentence
in the former decision of the Court, where it was said that
the Court need not go into the question how far the presidential power would reach in the event that a state had
neglected its duties, because this had not been the case in

Prussia. Papen and Kerrl used their majority on the three-man board, as changed by the presidential decree, immediately to dissolve the Diet and to order new elections for the fifth of March.

The Case Rests

Although the democratic parties agreed that here Hitler had violated the Constitution, and flagrantly so, the matter did not seem to present a good starting point for an uprising that could only be hopeless. There were some elements in this Prussian question that made it hard for the man in the street to understand it, now even more so than half a year before. A fight for Prussia's political independence, with the democrats fighting for Prussia and Hitler for the Reich; a fight for states' rights that failed to include the Prussian government's claim for police power—the only matter in which the anti-Hitler masses were interested at that moment—since the police was admittedly at the disposal of the Reich President in an emergency; a fight against popular elections for the continuation of a deadlocked legislature—these issues offered no attractive democratic objectives for a life-and-death struggle. The Prussian cabinet could, however, appeal to the Supreme State Court and try to obtain a statement that they had not been faithless to their constitutional duties, but that Hitler had been to his; and to get an injunction to prevent elections from being held in Prussia on the date set by Hitler.

It was not difficult to draw up an effective appeal. Yet it proved impossible to attain a decision prior to 5 March. Exchange of briefs and other procedural factors, the Court said, put it beyond their power to hold the hearing and to hand down the decision so soon. When counsel for Prussia protested that after the elections it would be too late to turn the tide, the justices, though well-intentioned, shrugged their shoulders. They were judges dealing with events of the past according to orderly procedure, and were no politicians.

Actually the apprehensions of the Prussian representative proved correct. The case never came to the final stage of an open hearing. After the elections, and after the flight of the Prussian prime minister to Switzerland and the ensuing resignation of the other ministers, the judicial procedure came to a technical stage of 'rest,' which meant that it rested until one of the parties to the conflict should take it up. In procedural language it is still resting today.

XI

Consequences of a Fire

Suspension of Individual Rights

ON 27 FEBRUARY THE REICHSTAG BUILDING WAS SET ON FIRE. A half-idiotic man was caught, Marinus van der Lubbe, who confessed to having committed the crime. The official report proclaimed that he had acted at the instigation and with the active help of the Communist Party, and the government immediately struck at the Communists with every means at its disposal.

Among the first steps taken, Hitler on the following morning elicited a presidential decree, by which the power given the President expressly in Article 48 of the Constitution was used to suspend all constitutional guarantees of individual liberty. The President could do this with ministerial countersignature in order to restore public peace and order whenever, according to his judgment, they were considerably disturbed or endangered. The technical meaning of such a decree was that the police could arrest and detain persons, search and seize property, suppress or censor newspapers, disband associations and prohibit public meetings, without any specific legal warrants and without judicial control. Article 117 of the Constitution, which in general terms guaranteed the inviolability of the person, was among the articles that could be suspended.[1]

This broad presidential power had been used before, especially by President Friedrich Ebert in various critical

[1] See Appendix D.

periods immediately after the War, for a few weeks or months on each occasion, under the control of the Reichstag then in session, and with the countersignature of Chancellors who were supported or tolerated by majorities. There were, however, two great differences between those earlier decrees and that of 28 February, apart from the absence of the legislature and the extended duration of the new decree.

A Dreadful Omission

Whenever Ebert suspended the constitutional guarantees of individual rights he always included in his decrees a paragraph that revived the old Protective Custody Act, enacted by the Reichstag during the War in 1916. This statute provided that an interned person must be heard before an ordinary court within twenty-four hours after his arrest; that he was entitled to have legal counsel who could inspect all records; and that he could appeal to some special board, which was authorized to set him free at any time and without whose previous consent he could not be detained for more than three months. The board could grant the person arrested compensation out of treasury funds, and was pledged to do so if it opined that the detention had not been necessary for the safety of the realm. This board, during the monarchical period, had been the Military Supreme Court, composed of judges and officers. During Ebert's term it had been made up of civilians only. The decree of 28 February 1933 for the first time since 1916 failed to provide for these controls, which ought long before to have been incorporated in the Constitution.

This omission implied the most dreadful consequences. It meant, legally speaking, that there was no limitation to what the National Socialist police could do with persons they considered detrimental to that kind of public peace and order which they wished to establish. The police could arrest such persons and extend the time of detention indefinitely. They could leave the relatives without any information regarding the prisoner's whereabouts and fate. They could prevent any lawyer or other person from visiting him or from looking into the records. They could treat him as they thought fit, e.g. overload him with work unsuited to him, feed and house him badly, force him to say formulae or to sing songs he detested, maltreat him in order to get him to confess or to divulge the names and acts of others; and, in case of breach of discipline or break-down of nerve, whip him, or shoot him. They could, 'to restore order in the camp,' punish him even for acts committed not by him but by his companions in prison. They could do all this, provided only their superiors allowed them to do so. And withal they could prevent the prisoner from communicating with any court, board, or other institution of review. The outside world, therefore, might hear nothing of what happened to the victim. No court would find the case on its dockets. No court had legal authority to take action, or any legal remedy, even if information reached the judge unofficially. There was no injunction, no writ of *habeas corpus, mandamus,* or the like that the Court could issue once the guarantee of individual rights was suspended. For that suspension freed the police not only from the limitations set by the Constitution itself but quite directly also from those established by statutes, such as the Code of Criminal Procedure and the Press Act. The leading commentators of the Constitution and the Supreme Court had always agreed on this point.

Such were the legal implications of the failure in the President's decree of 28 February to refer to the Protective Custody Act or to insert any other limitation to the powers of the police. Hindenburg was probably not aware of the omission when he signed the decree, and certainly not of its legal implications. Yet one cannot overstate the importance of this difference between the February decree of 1933 and former suspensions of individual rights by President Ebert.

The Police Receives Orders Not to Be Impartial

Secondly, the understanding in former emergency decrees of this kind was that the police, freed of judicial interference, should proceed impartially against *any* violation of the peace no matter from which side it came. This view, always hard to enforce, was now expressly abandoned. Hermann Göring, in charge of the Prussian police, issued regulations which admonished the police that the decree was not meant to suppress Nationalists but Communists, 'in defense against the communistic diatribes that have revealed their full dangerousness only at the very last moment and in order ruthlessly to eliminate that source of danger.' There were some allusions to the effect that those also were included who 'co-operated' with the Communists. On the other hand it was stated expressly that the police should not apply the decree against members of the Rightist organizations. 'In order to prevent blunders I call your attention to the fact that no measures based on the decree of 28 February must be taken against members of any parties or organizations unless they are Communists, Anarchists, or Social Democrats, except in cases where such measures serve in the broadest sense to fend off communistic activities. In other cases the decree of 4 February is to be applied.' The meaning of this exhortation was clear. Do not dare, thus the police were told by their superior, to interfere by virtue of the new decree with the 'National Revolution.' As to the former decree of 4 February, it did not suspend individual rights and judicial control in general terms, and Göring's regulation of 10 February concerning even that earlier decree had contained the following clause: 'The decree has not been issued to hinder those sections of the people who are backing the Government of the National Uprising, in

lending their welcome and necessary co-operation to the promotion of the Government's high aims.'

All Communist candidates were arrested in pursuance of
the new decree. Votes could be cast for them, and as many
as 12.3 per cent did fall to them, despite the persecutions, as
compared with 16.9 per cent in the preceding November
elections. Yet the newly elected members could not appear
when the House met, and the House, constitutionally entitled
to ask for the liberation of imprisoned members, did not so
demand. Since, according to the leading commentators, the
Constitution did not forbid arrests between dissolution and
elections, its letter was not violated.

Who Set the Fire?

The Reichstag fire, then, played a major role in precipi-
tating events. The National Socialists drew several advantages
from it. Not only did it give them the pretext for the final
blow to the Communist Party; it provided their police ministers with the broadest presidential powers ever given the
police, powers that to this day are formally derived from
Hindenburg's decree of 28 February 1933, which has never
been repealed. And it scared millions of voters away from the
Leftist parties or from a state of neutrality as non-voters,
causing them to give their votes to the National Socialists,
who protected them from Communism.

True, rumors cropped up immediately that National Socialists had staged the fire themselves. Yet only a small part
of the people was convinced beyond doubt that these rumors
were true. It was too fantastic for orderly and law-abiding
citizens to think that men who had just invoked God's blessing in the cabinet's solemn Proclamation should be so base
as to use such a diabolic device, and that afterwards they
should even be so brazen as to bring the case before the
Supreme Court, and in public speeches on every occasion and

with all signs of deep indignation to denounce the depravity
of those who spread such rumors. Said Göring, in the very
first words with which he opened the newly elected Reichstag four weeks later: 'An execrable crime has forced us to
move from the edifice that was erected "For The German
People." A political plot has destroyed its plenary chamber.
All of us know what motives drove a party, hostile to the
state, to commit that outrage.' And he thanked the Chancellor for the restoration of principles of 'honesty' and 'cleanli-
ness.' In his ensuing address, Hitler said: 'The Reichstag fire,
this failure of an attempt to start a general uprising, is only
a symptom of what Europe would have to expect from this
devilish doctrine of destruction. When in line with the political falsehood that has been raised to the rank of a principle
by Communism a certain press, especially abroad, now tries
to identify Germany's National Uprising with that out-
rageous action, it can only confirm my determination to leave
nothing untried to expiate this crime by the public execution
of the guilty incendiary and his accomplices within the short-
est time.' In the same address he spoke of the cabinet 'that
sees in Christianity the unshakable basis of our nation's ethical
and moral life.'

It is beyond the competence of this writer to establish the
true facts about the conflagration, and it is also beyond the
purpose of the present discussion, which deals with the second
stage of the fight against Fascism in Germany, to analyze
material that was later published abroad. For that material,
whatever its value, was not known to the German people
at that time. Historically interesting as the question is whether
criminal National Socialists, and which of them, had a hand
in the matter, it is only a point of secondary importance. Had
the eternal principles of Christianity, to which the cabinet
referred in its proclamation and Hitler in his speech, been
recognized by National Socialist ideology and practice, there

would have been no Totalitarian Fascism in Germany, and no need for a fight against it. The leading doctrine of the party, however, was that 'right is what is of use to the German people.' This maxim, unless limited by general ethical norms, makes any 'devilish' manœuvres appear right, including the hypocritical denial that they have been resorted to, whenever the leading group considers them useful for the German people. In line with this principle, so often extolled by them, National Socialists *could* have staged the fire and *could* still have denied it afterwards in the manner they did, if they regarded that useful for the people—or even, if they only thought it useful for the victory of the party, since that was understood to be useful for the people. An unethical doctrine rather than the deed of criminal individuals is at stake.

As has been said above, the great majority of the people did not believe that the National Socialists had actually set the fire, although many observers were aware that the principle just mentioned made this possible. A great many people, perhaps even half the population, were inclined to believe the charge against the Communists, however strange it was to think that the Communists should have chosen the destruction of the Reichstag building for a demonstration against the National Socialists, who themselves had always been hostile to parliamentary debates. Others postponed final judgment in regard to the origin of the fire.

Later on the Supreme Court acquitted the accused Communists. A former National Liberal, one time republican prime minister of Saxony, Dr. Bünger, was the presiding judge. Obviously the Court, too, failed to take the rumors seriously that the National Socialists had staged the fire. The justices considered it, so to speak, beneath the dignity of the Court to admit such a suspicion against the government. Yet they had the courage, and courage it required, to dismiss the indictment against the Communists despite the propaganda and the urgent demands on the part of the authorities.

The acquittal, however, pronounced in December, came much too late to offset the increase in power that the fire had procured for the National Socialists. We must now, therefore, return to the elections of 5 March.

XII

The Snare of the Fowler

Error, Guilt, or Reasonable Choice?

EVEN UNDER SUCH PRESSURE THE ELECTIONS YIELDED NO MA-
jority for the National Socialist Party. They did, however,
provide a fair majority for it in combination with the German Nationals, and even without them when the Communists
were not counted.

Thereupon Hitler took the next step by demanding an
enabling act that gave him full power to act regardless of the
legal limits to the powers of the executive branch as set down
in the Constitution. He threatened that if this power were not
granted he would be unable to halt the revolutionary torrent
and the irregular acts of violence and terror that were sweeping the country.

Any enabling act was considered technically valid under
the Constitution when it obtained a two-thirds majority in
both houses. That majority and no more was required for
any change, no matter how fundamental it might be, according to the prevailing opinion of the courts, the lawyers, and
the commentators.

The assent of the second chamber composed of the representatives of the several states was assured, since most of them
had come meanwhile under National Socialist command directly or indirectly. In the Reichstag, however, Hitler could
obtain two-thirds in an unquestionable fashion only if the
Catholic Center would vote for the bill. On 23 March, the
Catholics did indeed do so, bringing the majority up to 444

votes of Yes against the 94 Noes of the Social Democrats. This was far more than the required two-thirds majority, and would have been so even if the 81 Communists and 26 Social Democrats who were absent because of arrest, death, flight abroad, or illness had been present and had added their ballots to the No-votes. If the Center Party had voted against the Act the figures would have been very different. Even then two-thirds might have been reached in appearance, but merely so because those more than one hundred Communists and Social Democrats were prevented by force from attending the meeting. The Act's moral authority and technical legitimacy then could have been questioned anywhere at any time.

The legalistic disguise of the sliding revolution reached its final stage with this passage of the Enabling Act of 23 March. Why, then, did the Catholic Center not use its numerical strength to frustrate the attempt to get it passed with a large majority? Why did a party that had so much to fear for its ideals and interests from National Socialism assist in the materialization of Hitler's boldest dreams of dictatorial power acquired under the guise of right and justice? There was not one among them who voted against the Act or who, although present at the meeting, abstained from voting. Even Brüning cast his vote for it.

One has tried to find the explanation for this baffling action —outstanding in the long series of abortive attempts at a policy of appeasement—in personal frailty or treason, in backstage bargaining or bribery. Never would the entire party, never a man like Brüning, have cast their votes on such grounds, even if a number of members had. The true explanation is contained in the party's conception of the alternative. They believed, and with good reason, that if they refused to vote for the measure the revolution would go ahead on illegal roads, starting with an orgy of cruelty and bloodshed. Their consent, so they hoped, might avoid such disaster. Confronted with the choice between Hitler and his most extreme followers, they preferred giving Hitler *limited* powers to his obtaining unlimited ones by a victory of his radical adherents, who would present a bill of their own.

Five Safety Valves for Liberty

Five clauses of limitation were written into the Enabling Act to obtain the consent of the non-Nazis to it. First, the delegated power was given not to Hitler personally, but to his existing cabinet. The Act was to go out of force automatically 'when the present cabinet is replaced by another.' This, the Catholics argued, would leave vital decisions in the hands of non-Nazis, who held more than two-thirds of the cabinet posts. Secondly, the power was limited to four years: the Act was to lose its force automatically on 1 April 1937. Thirdly, fourthly, and fifthly, the power was limited by clauses that declared invalid any deviations from the Weimar Constitution 'if they had as their subject the institutions of the Reichstag or of the Reichsrat as such,' or if they impaired the constitutional 'rights of the Reich President.' Among the presidential rights was that to dismiss the Chancellor at any time, and to hold the supreme command of the Army. The aggregate of these clauses, so it was argued, set up important counterbalances against despotism. Should the Catholic Center vote against this Bill, they were sure the very next day would see Hitler's elevation to absolute power by a revolutionary act with all checks and balances omitted.

The Enabling Act, therefore, was not exactly a *lex regia*, i.e. a Royal Law that transferred the supreme power to one man. On the other hand, it included no guarantees of individual rights. When England's Henry VIII prevailed upon the Commons to pass the Statute of Proclamations in 1539, the House forced him to substitute for his original bill a new

one which specifically excepted from the king's proclamations the 'inheritances, lawful possessions, offices, liberties,
privileges, franchises, goods, or chattels' of subjects.[1] Hitler
definitely refused to give such guarantees in legal language.
However, the other members of the cabinet and Hindenburg
retained the legal power to prevent arbitrary encroachments
on individual rights. A change in the majority of the cabinet
would automatically obligate all courts and civil servants to
refuse obedience to cabinet decrees. The spokesman of the
Catholic Center, prelate Kaas, expressed the apprehensions of
his friends regarding individual rights, but he found some
cause for hope, supported by the references to Christian principles and other conciliatory remarks made by Hitler in the
course of the debate. The handful of Liberals—the State
Party, as the Democrats now called themselves, and the German People's Party—followed the lead of the Center. So did
its sister party of Bavarian Catholics.

Courage of the Socialists

Only the members of the Social Democratic Party voted
against the Act, no matter what they thought the alternative
was. All the 94 present did. Some of those absent were under
arrest. Some had been maltreated. Others had left the country
to avoid certain imprisonment, maltreatment, or death, or to
organize resistance from outside. In view of the acts of violence that, unrestrained by the police, went on against anyone
who incurred the wrath of the Storm Troops or of irregular
Nazi gangs, it required great courage to go to the Reichstag
meeting to vote against the Enabling Act. It required extraordinary courage to mount the rostrum after Hitler had finished
and to say what Otto Wels, the leader of the Social Democratic Party, then said:

[1] For details see C. H. McIlwain, *Constitutionalism, Ancient and Modern*,
1940, p. 109.

No blessing can come from a peace imposed by violence; even less in domestic [than in foreign] affairs. No genuine national community can be founded on it. May the Cabinet protect themselves from crude excesses of polemics, may they place instigations to, and acts of, violence under penalty of the law. That may be done, if it is carried through equally and impartially in every direction, and if one keeps from treating defeated adversaries as though they were outlaws.

One can take our freedom and our lives, but not our honor . . . After the persecution that the Social Democratic Party has experienced lately, no one can fairly demand and expect that they will vote for the Enabling Act as here introduced . . .

Never since there has been a German Reichstag [i.e. since 1871] has the control of public affairs by the elected representatives of the people been eliminated to such an extent as it is at present and as it will be still further under the new Enabling Act . . .

Our achievements in the reconstruction of the country and its economy and in the liberation of the occupied territory will stand the judgment of history. We have established equal rights for all, and a social labor law. We have helped to create a Germany in which the road to state leadership is open not only to princes and barons but also to men of the working class . . .

The attempt to turn back the wheel of history will fail. We Social Democrats know that mere protests cannot do away with facts that are based on power politics [*machtpolitische Tatsachen*]. We do see that in terms of power politics your rule is an actual fact at present. *Yet the people's sense of justice [Rechtsbewusstsein, consciousness of right and wrong] is a political power, too,* and we shall never cease to appeal to it.

The Weimar Constitution is no socialist constitution. However, we stand by the principles of a government based on law and justice [*Rechtsstaat*], of equality of rights, and of social law, as therein established. We German Social Democrats, in this historic hour, confess to the principles of humanity and justice, of freedom and socialism. *No enabling act can give you the power to destroy ideas that are eternal and indestructible.*

We salute those who are persecuted and oppressed. We salute our friends everywhere in the country. Their steadfastness and loyalty deserve admiration. Their courage of confession, their unbroken faith, are guarantees of a brighter future.

Wels, after the meeting, managed to escape across the frontier. Driven from country to country he died in exile. Not so fortunate was the former leader of the Prussian Social Democrats, Ernst Heilmann. He was soon taken to a concentration camp, and died there after years of suffering.

Consequences of the Enabling Act

Open political fight against the full victory of totalitarian ideas was restricted to narrow limits after the passage of the Enabling Act. Leaders of the Social Democrats could no longer be active. They had four choices open to them. They could try to leave the country. Many did so, like Otto Braun and his colleague Otto Klepper, liberal minister of finance in the Prussian cabinet, and many thousands before and after them, including the Catholic ex-chancellor Heinrich Brüning and his cabinet colleague, Gottfried R. Treviranus of the Conservative People's Party, both of whom left Germany in 1934, escaping the Blood Purge.

Those who could not or would not flee could commit suicide. Many did, beginning with Toni Pfülf, woman member of the Social Democratic Reichstag Party, because they could not endure passively to watch what was happening to their ideals. *Grauen* (horror) killed them.

They could defy the National Socialists in some open fashion, and thus bring upon themselves the martyrdom that followed. Many did, first among them Wilhelm Sollmann, Cologne's Socialist deputy to the Reichstag, a few days after the March elections. They were taken to some 'brown house,' cellar or concentration camp, and maltreated. Sometimes such

treatment was considered irregular, and the victim was released as was the case with Sollmann, who escaped to Luxem-
bourg the following day and is now in the United States. But
others, less fortunate, were systematically trained to obedience in the camps, or eventually put to death or driven to
suicide there.

Many were interned because of defiant actions they had
committed before the Nazis came to power, like Johannes
Stelling, one of the senior members of the Reichstag Social
Democratic Party, who was a dead man a few days after his
arrest, or the Prussian socialist Ernst Heilmann, who perished
more slowly, and two younger members of the party, Kurt
Schumacher and Dr. Carl Mierendorff, both war veterans, as
was Heilmann too. It was not always a matter of choice,
therefore, whether to take the thorny way that led to a concentration camp. But even when it was, the end was either
submission to at least the external behavior of obedience, or
to death. Often no one would hear anything of the act of
defiance itself. News of it would be suppressed. No meaning-
ful political effect, then, could seem to result from taking
this third road, but only deeper humiliation for those who
did.

There was finally the choice of withdrawal from all action
and of living quietly under close police surveillance. A number of political leaders chose this road, after they had done
their part earlier. Among them was the former Prussian minister Carl Severing, surprisingly allowed to live on in this
fashion, and the former Reichstag President, Paul Löbe. The
slightest move on their part of political opposition or conspiracy with others would send them to a concentration
camp, much more quickly than anybody else.

The choices left to outspoken Liberals were hardly different. If it was still possible to prevent the rise of full-fledged

Totalitarianism, others than Social Democrats and Liberals would have to do the fighting.

The Jews, of course, could not do this either, although in Berlin and some other places they were safer in their homes and activities at first than were socialist and liberal leaders. Not until the first of April was action taken against them on a nation-wide scale by way of a one-day boycott ordained by the party and tolerated by the government. That demonstration, sinister as it was, may now appear relatively harmless as compared with what followed later. Many indeed hoped it was the final token payment for the much more brutal demands of the party, designed to let them simmer down to avert a violent outbreak. But at the same time most people were aware that the German Jews were the great hostages of the new regime. Any shot fired at its leaders, any attempted revolt, would be horribly revenged on the Jews. Many a plan of anti-Nazi action was abandoned, at that time as well as later on, for this reason. Few observers abroad have ever realized how much this thought paralyzed action at a time when action technically may have been possible.

At any rate, no Liberal, no Social Democrat, no Communist, and no Jew, and no other person known to the government as a possible enemy, could engage in any open political struggle against Totalitarianism. The only way that such struggles could be continued openly seemed to be 'mitigating collaboration' with the new regime, i.e. collaboration with the aim of averting totalitarian abuses.

Thus the political tug-of-war between Conservatives and non-political Christian forces, on the one hand, and extreme National Socialists on the other became the only feature of the open political scene. The rest of the people were still for a few months struggling for some political rights. They practically had no way of open political expression left to them, even before these rights were legally abolished.

XIII

The Civil Service and the Courts

Error, Guilt, or Duty?

THE ENABLING ACT PLACED THE ESTABLISHMENTS OF THE Civil Service and of the courts at the disposal of the Hitler cabinet for whatever it deemed fit to decree. Courts and civil servants probably would have fought loyally against a revolution that did not come to them in legalistic disguise. Led by the permanent under-secretaries they had done so to a remarkable extent during the Kapp Putsch in 1920, although that early revolt was animated by conservative ideas much more popular among the permanent officials than were the fascist ideas of Hitler's party. Many would have done so again if confronted with a clear violation of law and Constitution by Hitler acting like Kapp as a usurper.

Yet after Hitler's constitutional appointment by the legitimate Reich President and the passage of the Enabling Act by the majority required in the Constitution, there seemed to civil servants and judges no choice as officials but to obey. Not only had they to submit to manifest power, but their very professional duty seemed to demand that they apply decrees, if issued within the limits of the Enabling Act, regardless of any positive or negative approval they might feel. The individual public employee could, of course, withdraw and starve. If he stayed in office, he could warn and advise during the preparation stage of new measures. He could try to mitigate their execution as far as possible. Yet once a decree on the basis of the Enabling Act had been issued, he had to execute it, if execution fell under his jurisdiction.

Actually, the execution of morally objectionable measures rarely fell within the jurisdiction of the permanent officials, few of whom had anything to do with them. Terroristic methods, such as the training of opponents to obedience in concentration camps, or in later years the expulsion of Jews, were not left to the regular civil servants but entrusted to party organizations. The supervisory officers in the police ministries were dismissed and new ones picked either from outside or from the relatively small number of those leading civil servants that had proved themselves to be genuine National Socialists. The great mass of civil servants was glad to have 'morally neutral' functions, such as dealing with economic affairs, tax collection, social security, statistics, postal or railroad service, foreign currency, municipal government or its supervision, and the like, which did not imply acts that they judged to be immoral and unethical. If indirectly such questions entered their jurisdiction, e.g. if they had to apply discriminating financial measures, they could try to be fair to the victims in details within the boundaries of the law. Being of such service brought some moral comfort to the civil servants in these years. Matters would only become worse if they left office, they would say.

Positivism and Professional Ethics

The judges, too, would consider it their professional duty to apply the decree-laws issued under the Enabling Act, even if they deeply disapproved of them. This was the ultimate effect, indeed a most challenging consequence, of the unlimited doctrine of positivism, nourished by the lawyers in all western countries. The lawyer, so this doctrine says, has to apply the constitution and the law as they stand. He may check a law with regard to a written constitution where there is one, but no judge is permitted to apply his own ideas of justice and higher law in contradiction to written statutes that are in line with the constitution. This formidable doc-trine made it even a matter of 'professional ethics' for the judges not to supplant the decree-laws of Hitler's cabinet—technically 'valid' under the Constitution—with the higher-law opinions of the indignant judge. It is desirable that a deeper analysis than that customary during the last century should lead lawyers and political scientists to revise their ex-treme positivism and to think once more of principles that are so holy and fundamental that any judge should apply them at any time even against the technically valid commands of his government. Yet this is a very controversial issue among lawyers, if it is at all controversial in view of the pre-vailing positivistic doctrine. It would seem that supra-national constitutions, directly binding upon judges and administra-tors in all member states, can alone help us out of the traps or unlimited positivism.[1]

Exactly as the administrative employees, the ordinary courts in Germany had but little to do with fascist methods. The February decree excluded police measures from their control. Therefore, instead of bringing a matter before the ordinary courts, the National Socialist police ministers were always free to take their victims to a concentration camp, from which they could not appeal. Thus the courts would not find such cases on their dockets. Or the police could transfer a prisoner to a concentration camp after he had served his term in jail, if the police considered that term too short. Cases of high treason against the regime were taken out of the ordinary courts and turned over to a special Peo-ple's Court, composed of reliable party adherents.

[1] See Arnold Brecht, 'Limited-Purpose Federations,' *Social Research*, vol. 10 (1943), pp. 135-51; 'European Federation—The Democratic Alternative,' *Harvard Law Review*, vol. 55 (1942), pp. 561-94; and 'Distribution of Powers Between an International Government and the Governments of National States,' *American Political Science Review*, vol. 37 (1943), pp. 862-72.

Within the remaining narrow limits, the judges in Germany have behaved more courageously than is generally known. They often defied the Nazi prosecutors by acquitting accused persons, or by setting the penalty at its legal minimum. They have refused to acknowledge inconclusive evidence, have interpreted incriminating remarks in a harmless way, or have found ways and means to alleviate the legal implications. Only future research will fully reveal the number of such cases, and also to what extent judges have failed to lend their help when they might have done so. That many judges have shown courage could hardly be better demonstrated than by Hitler's outburst against them in his Reichstag speech on 26 April 1942. There he gave examples of mild sentences passed by German courts and said, according to *The New York Times:*

The front, the homeland, the transport system *and judiciary* must be governed by one single idea to achieve victory. No one can hope to insist upon his well-acquired rights. I therefore ask the German Reichstag for an explicit endorsement of my legal right to demand of every one the discharge of his duties or to cashier any one from his post or office if I consider that he has failed in his duty, regardless of who he may be or what acquired right he may have . . . Judges who do not recognize the commands of the hour will be removed from office. In this time there are no self-satisfied people with well-deserved privileges. We are all obedient servants to the common interests of the nation.[2]

Hitler's repeated and angry references to the notion of 'well-acquired rights'[3] showed that his attempts to remove

[2] *The New York Times,* 27 April 1942, p. 4. Said Raymond Daniell in his comment from London in the same issue, 'It would appear that at least part of the Reich's judiciary has been asserting its right to be independent within a limit.'

[3] 'Well-acquired rights' (*Wohlerworbene Rechte*) is a concept used in the Weimar Constitution to characterize those rights of judges and other officials that were protected from interference. One of the clauses in Article

or discipline judges had met with the objection that judges were independent in the exercise of their judicial functions and could be removed against their will only by the decision of courts composed of other regular judges, and only because of neglect of their legal duties. The one-party Reichstag, at Hitler's request, passed a special act, amending the Constitution, which gave Hitler the power to disregard the independence of judges and their acquired rights, and he directed his minister of justice to see to it that full co-ordination was achieved. It is remarkable that this incident occurred as late as 1942.

The Sliding Revolution

To come back to the initial period of the Hitler regime, the one road left to the individual civil servant and judge besides that of executing the cabinet's decree legislation was that of retirement. If all of them, with one accord, had retired on the same day, it would have been a formidable blow, perhaps even a deadly one, to the new regime. Yet there was no date, during the first few months at least, that brought a *governmental* action so challenging that, without any previous agreement, all civil servants with their widely diversified individual opinions could have risen in protest on the same day. The legalistic disguises of the fascist regime precluded such an automatic display of resistance. In order to *agree* on a joint policy and on a date for its execution, it would have been necessary to discuss the situation. Yet there was left no possibility for such discussion. 'Conspiracies' of that kind would have been nipped in the bud.

Hence there was no possibility of concerted action. A number of civil servants withdrew individually, yet at different times. Some volunteered in offering their services to the constitutional cause when Papen drove the Prussian ministers out

129 read: 'The well-acquired rights of the officials [*Beamte*] are inviolable.' Article 102 stated: 'Judges are independent and subject only to the law.'

of office, and they did so again when Hitler repeated that manœuvre. Others retired after Hitler's appointment, or when a new decree was passed that was offensive to their fundamental principles, or when they had to apply such a decree. Some defied the party by positive action, such as the ministerial counsellor, Walter Wüllenweber, who—himself non-Jewish—entered several Jewish shops conspicuously on the day of the boycott, suffering the consequences first of a furlough and later of dismissal. Such independent acts did not endanger the regime. On the contrary, through the decree-law of 7 April 1933 the cabinet itself took action toward the dismissal of 'unreliable' and Jewish governmental employees.

Not all Jews were dismissed at that early time. Those appointed prior to the First World War and those who had participated in a battle stayed on in office, even in judgeships, until the end of 1935. Those dismissed received their regular pensions. Persons considered 'unreliable,' whether Jew or Gentile, had their pensions curtailed by one-fourth but received the rest. Pensions for all those who had not gone through the normal career service were revised or canceled. When Jewish war veterans were forced out in 1935, they kept their full salaries for several years, as if they were still in office. The definite change to the worse did not occur until the end of 1938.

Expressed in percentages of the entire Civil Service, the number of dismissals appears small. But if the higher ranks are considered separately, the result looks different. Out of 1663 Prussian members of the higher Civil Service in field positions as many as 469, i.e. 28 per cent, were either dismissed as 'unreliable,' Jewish or the like (12.5 per cent), or dismissed or demoted to lower positions for 'administrative reasons' (15.5 per cent). Figures of dismissals at headquarters are not available. In the middle brackets of the Civil Service, including especially the clerical class, only 3.46 per cent were affected (unreliable, etc., 1.13 per cent; for other reasons, 2.33 per cent).[4]

These figures do not, however, justify the inference that all of those who remained in office were National Socialists. The great majority were certainly not, especially not at that early time. They stayed and were allowed to stay, because their functions were politically neutral, exactly as those who were demoted on the ground that they were not Nazis would stay in their new positions in order not to starve. They constituted no danger to National Socialism, since the legalistic disguises of the new regime made them sufficiently reliable as administrators in non-political posts. Rather, their dismissal would have endangered the regime.

All those officials that had to deal with political action, or personnel questions, including the regional and district presidents (*Oberpräsidenten, Regierungspräsidenten*), county directors (*Landräte*), police presidents, and their principal aides, were actually affected by the changes in personnel, with a very few, if any, exceptions in favor of incumbents who appeared acceptable to the new regime even in such positions. Many other public employees joined the party in subsequent years. Some agencies, such as the Foreign Office, did so *in corpore*, in order to preclude discriminations according to the party status of the individual employee. But even so the official Civil Service Association stated that as late as 1939 only 350,000 of its 1.5 million members, that is, 28.2 per cent, were party members.[5] These figures included those of persons appointed after 1933.

[4] Figures established by the Research Project of the Graduate Faculty, New School for Social Research, on Postwar Germany. In addition it is said that 60,000 members of the police force were later taken over by the Army. Their police positions were given to new appointees.

[5] *Deutsches Beamten Jahrbuch* 1939, p. 171.

Character of the German Civil Servants

To this day, the individual persons who in their aggregate constitute the German Civil Service and Judiciary are widely diversified in their views regarding political, economic, and social questions. Their ideals range all the way from the belief in a strictly authoritarian form of government, through the more traditional faith in some kind of constitutionally limited authoritarian rule, to a nostalgia for democracy. From personal loyalty to Hitler and lip service given the present regime, to the tacit performing of daily duties by the majority, and frank statements of fundamental differences in principles and value judgments by quite a few. From belief in command economy through that in liberal economy, to the hope for some kind of democratic and ethical socialism. From feudal standards of political, social, and economic differentiations, to extreme equalitarianism. And in the educational field, from the guidance by established Protestant and Catholic churches to the complete separation of state and church in the American and, formerly, French way. It would be foolish to believe that in all these respects the German civil servants had uniform ideas and predilections at the end of the democratic period or that they have them now.

Yet it can safely be said that the following criteria are common to the overwhelming majority, at least of those who entered the Civil Service prior to 1933. They would welcome the restoration in German policy of ethical principles in line with Christian and humanitarian traditions. This tendency prevails especially with regard to the methods applied in the persecution of the Jews and the use made of concentration camps and unusual forms of punishment. Furthermore, practically all the members of the old Civil Service have the ideal in common that judicial independence should be restored. More, they wish for the restoration of what the Germans call

Rechtsstaat, i.e. a state in which every individual is certain that he will be dealt with by the public authorities not in an arbitrary manner, but only according to pre-established law and subject to principles the application of which is under the supervision of independent judges or courtlike boards, such as independent administrative courts.

It is further safe to say that to this day the older civil servants and judges—those appointed before 1933—are opposed to the principle that every action should be considered right if good for the German nation. They would either reject this National Socialist maxim, or accept it only with the understanding that no violation of basic ethical principles is good for the German nation. To this day practically all of them oppose the idea that right is what some party or group thinks to be good for Germany without regard to ethical standards.

It is probable that a considerable part of the younger members of the Civil Service does not think differently from their elders in these matters.

On the other hand, practically all members of the Civil Service, whether young or old, are at one in believing that for a considerable time no regime in Germany will be able to go on without a great amount of regulation in both the economic and political spheres.

Only someone who is well acquainted with the German civil servants is able to estimate the torment through which many of them have gone since Hitler's access to power.

XIV

The Curtain Falls—14 July 1933

Period of Technical 'Legality'

EXCEPT FOR THE STEP TAKEN AGAINST THE PRUSSIAN CABINET on 6 February, there was perhaps no overt governmental measure during the first five months that from a purely legalistic point of view constituted a flagrant violation of the written law. The limits set by the Enabling Act were being strictly observed in this second stage of the fight. They did not prevent the cabinet from abolishing the permanent tenure of civil servants or the independence of judges, from discriminating against Jews, from disbanding the trade unions, from prohibiting emigration without a special permit, and the like. All this and more was possible under the Enabling Act. If conservative cabinet members did ever object to any of these measures, they failed either to vote against them or, at least, to establish the fact publicly that a majority in the cabinet had so voted. If Hindenburg ever objected, he did not dismiss the Chancellor. Thus, formal legality was being maintained. Not until 7 July 1933, when the cabinet deprived all Social Democrats of their seats in the Reichstag, and more definitely a week later, when on 14 July the cabinet outlawed all political parties, except that of the National Socialists, did a decree clearly trespass on forbidden grounds.

Open Violation of Oath and Pledges

The decree-law of 14 July, which deserves much closer attention than it has generally received, reads:

Sec. 1. In Germany, the National Socialist German Workers Party is the only political party.

Sec. 2. Whoever attempts to preserve the organization of any other political party, or to form a new political party, shall be punished with hard labor [*Zuchthaus*] of not more than three years or with imprisonment [*Gefängnis*] of not less than six months and not more than three years.

The outlawing of all parties except the one under the command of Hitler violated the clause in the Enabling Act stating that no deviations from the Weimar Constitution should be valid that affected the institution of the Reichstag as such. A chamber that was to be constituted of members of one party alone, elected on the basis of nominations made by that party to the exclusion of any nominations from outside; party membership reserved to a small percentage of the people; all other parties outlawed and anyone attempting to form a new party threatened with hard labor and the concentration camp—such a chamber was no Reichstag in the sense of the Enabling Act, even if it were given that name. When the Enabling Act ordained that 'the institution of the Reichstag as such' could *not* be made the subject of any decree-law, it referred to a body in which the various opinions held by the German people were represented by members who, at least according to the written law, could be freely elected by the people, and in which controversial opinions could be freely expressed. It presupposed, therefore, either the continuation of the Reichstag then existing and elected for a constitutional term of four years, or the holding of new elections in which candidates of various views could offer their proposals and alternatives to the voters. A decree that restricted representation of the people to the one party that the Enabling Act wanted to see controlled, if ever so weakly, by the existence of the Reichstag actually had the institution of the Reichstag as its subject, and nothing else. This new decree was, therefore, invalid under the Enabling Act.

Consequences

All the carefully formulated clauses of the Enabling Act broke down with this one decree. Thereafter, a newly elected one-party 'Reichstag,' if considered as legitimate, could easily produce the two-thirds majority required for new amendments to the Constitution and for new enabling acts. So it happened. Using the first opportunity on 30 January 1934, the one-party Reichstag unanimously passed an act to abolish all sovereign state rights and to authorize the Reich cabinet without any limitation 'to make new constitutional law.' Two weeks later the Reich cabinet abolished the Federal Council (Reichsrat), therewith removing the second limitation set down in the Enabling Act. How careful Hitler and his advisers were to observe the letter of the law is illustrated by the fact that this interference with the 'institution of the Federal Council as such,' forbidden by the first Enabling Act, was based on a new constitutional amendment passed with all the technical requirements of the Weimar Constitution religiously observed. Accordingly, even the Federal Council's own consent to the abolition of state rights had been asked for and formally given, as all state governments were dominated by National Socialists.

When the four-year term for which the first Enabling Act had granted full powers was about to expire in 1937, great care was taken to have the 'Reichstag' pass a new amendment in due time to prolong its validity. Therewith the third of the limitations set in the first Enabling Act—the time limit—was removed expressly, although the act of 30 January 1934 had already done so implicitly.

A different procedure was used with regard to the rights of the President. After Hindenburg's death in 1934 Hitler might have held new presidential elections to have either himself or a puppet elected President. He preferred having the two offices of President and Chancellor combined. He did not leave the passage of this constitutional amendment to the Reichstag, but asked for a plebiscite. That plebiscites initiated by the cabinet could change the Constitution had been previously established by constitutional amendment. The plebiscite promptly yielded the desired result. Counter-proposals were, of course, not permitted in it. If the people had any choice at all it was between *two* National-Socialist heads—President and Chancellor—or *one*, the combined Chancellor-President. They genuinely preferred one. The plebiscite was held only a few weeks after Hitler, in the Blood Purge of 30 June 1934, had aroused new hopes that he would rid himself of the extreme and immoral elements in his party. For that had been the significance of the purge in the eyes of most German observers at that time. They did not care, and often did not even know, that many Conservative and Catholic opponents of Hitler also had been killed in the purge. They were dazzled by the fact that Hitler had risen to defend the traditional Army against the Storm Troops of the party, who wanted fusion with the Army; that he had exhibited 'statesmanship' in severing the bonds that had bound him to some of his oldest friends, such as Ernst Röhm, chief of the Storm Troops; that he had rushed to Munich personally to uncover their pernicious and immoral activities; that he seemed firm and severe on the question of immoral friendship between men; and that he did not hesitate even to have his old friends executed in order to carry through what appeared at that time to be a more moderate and ethical policy.

The Courts: 'Not on Their Dockets'

The legalistic implications of the decree of 14 July 1933 have generally been overlooked, because terror had practically eliminated the non-totalitarian parties even prior to the decree, and because the public is hardly interested in the technical forms of revolutionary legislation, failing to understand the great bearing of legalistic disguises on the attitude of civil servants and courts. The German judges, however, must have seen that the decree violated the Enabling Act. Why, then, did they not invalidate it? This question more perhaps than any other reflects upon the honor of the German judges.

Actually the validity of the decree has hardly ever come before the courts directly. It was not necessary for the Nazi attorneys to bring attempts to form a new party or maintain old party ties before the ordinary courts. There were other and more drastic means of preventing new political organizations from being formed and of suppressing any conspiracies against the regime. Indirectly the courts might have had cause to deal with the validity of the decree when they applied statutes issued in subsequent Reichstag acts. It would have been their duty to deny the validity of such acts, because the so-called Reichstag was not legitimate. There were, however, few such statutes, and those that were issued during the first three or four years were not concerned with matters that came before the courts. It was, on a larger scale, not unlike those questions in American practice that in spite of their dubious validity for more than a hundred years never came before the Supreme Court, e.g. whether the President could dismiss his Secretaries and other officers without the consent of the Senate.

Not until 1937, when the decree power was prolonged by the one-party Reichstag, were the courts definitely affected. Thereafter each decree passed by the cabinet could have been

challenged on the ground that the prolongation of the Enabling Act was invalid. Yet at that time it had practically become too late for any court to question Hitler's power on
constitutional grounds. A new sovereignty could be said to
have become a matter of fact meanwhile, and so to be no
longer challengeable by courts on the basis of the Weimar
Constitution. There was, alas! no theory of inalienable rights
and of necessary standards of justice outside the constitutional law left among the lawyers of the western world in the
twentieth century.

The Foreign Countries: 'Not Their Affair'

In criticizing civil servants and courts we should not for-
get that they were not the only ones that were paralyzed by
the legalistic disguise. The foreign countries, too, and their
ambassadors, bowed to the new regime. This is even more
surprising under the circumstances, because they were not
under the threat of concentration camps and death if they
refused to recognize the regime. Legal techniques that bound
domestic courts did not tie their hands. Had in the 1920's
William II one day returned to Germany to resume the
throne, the former Allies would certainly have intervened
immediately. When Hitler's party with its much more extreme principles assumed power, they acquiesced. This ac-
quiescence, in turn, confirmed the attitude of the public employees and courts. It seemed to imply that, even if the
formalistic view was discarded and the Weimar Constitution
regarded as violated, there was a new sovereignty, no longer
based on the Weimar Constitution but on revolutionary facts,
and legitimized by what legal and political theory in all countries and at all courts of the Western World considered the
most important factor, i.e. recognition by foreign countries.

The End

Thus on 14 July 1933—the anniversary of the day when the Bastille, sinister keep of political prisoners under France's absolute monarchy, was stormed—any organized opposition to the National Socialist Party by any group of persons in Germany was declared illegal. Thenceforth such opposition was prevented not merely through terroristic methods extra-legally applied by party organization; it was officially prohibited and outlawed by the government in power. Any objection was restricted to private warnings and advice, to struggles in the form of controversies among collaborating groups, or to religious disputes. Even these were tolerated only to such extent as they did not imply a political fight against the regime.

Totalitarianism, then, was firmly established. Open fight against it had come to an end. The curtain had fallen. The great silence reigned.

APPENDICES

Appendix A

The Fallacies of Intellectual History

PHILOSOPHICALLY MINDED OBSERVERS HAVE SOMETIMES SUC-
cumbed to grave fallacies in drawing from the intellectual
origin of National Socialism sweeping conclusions in regard
to the composition of the German people. They have singled
out undemocratic elements in the thought of poets, thinkers,
and statesmen through several centuries and have suggested
that this intellectual history reveals the totalitarian character
of the *people*. Interesting as any profound investigations into
the history of thought are for various other reasons, they
cannot, except with great caution, be used for an appraisal
of the ideas of the common man. The fact that certain ideas
have been expressed in prominent writings does not permit
us to say that they are characteristic of the popular thinking
at a definite time. Still less does the fact that they have served
as vehicles or camouflage for fascist and totalitarian propaganda demonstrate that they were themselves fascist and totalitarian.

Let us consider a few illustrations of both fallacies. All of
the following intellectual movements or ideas, most of them
not German in origin, have contributed to paving the intellectual road for Fascism and Totalitarianism: Machiavellian-
ism, as derived—rightly or wrongly—from Machiavelli's *The
Prince;* political and legal positivism, as proclaimed by Hobbes
and widely accepted by the legal profession later on; relativism, rising after 1900 in political and legal philosophy; [1] the

[1] See Arnold Brecht, 'The Rise of Relativism in Political and Legal
Philosophy' in *Social Research*, vol. 6 (1939), pp. 392-414; and 'The Myth
of Is and Ought' in *Harvard Law Review*, vol. 54 (1941), pp. 811-31.

glorification of violence by George Sorel in France, as superior to democratic bargaining; the realistic analysis of political action and success by Vilfredo Pareto; the praise of leadership by Charles Maurras; and the example set by Bolshevism for powerful one-party dictatorship. It would obviously be fallacious to infer from such interconnection of ideas that the present countrymen of Machiavelli, Hobbes, of the relativists, Sorel, Pareto and Maurras, not to speak of the Bolshevists, were inclined toward Fascism, and even more so to say how many were so inclined. We need other methods to find that out.

The second fallacy is like confusing the owner of a car with a driver who, with no title, uses it for his own dubious purposes. Hobbes, Sorel, and Pareto were neither fascists nor totalitarians, whatever else they may have been. Even Machiavelli was neither one nor the other, as more and more of his critics agree. If ideas of these writers were seized upon by the new regimes in Italy and Germany, this has not made the original authors fascist or totalitarian.

Both fallacies have been used abundantly with respect to German intellectual history. Among those who have from time to time been held spiritual ancestors of fascist and totalitarian thought in Germany are the following: Luther, because he stressed state authority in earthly matters; Kant, because he emphasized duty; Fichte, because he glorified the nation; Hegel, because he idealized the state; Nietzsche, because he despised rationalism; and even Goethe, because he praised order and inward freedom as the prerequisites to creative work above equalitarian justice and independence. We may rightly see political danger in some of these ideas and traditions and we do know that the National Socialists have employed them for their own purposes. Yet it would be a grave fallacy to call them in themselves fascist or totalitarian. The specific essentials of Fascism and Totalitarianism were fundamentally foreign to Luther, Kant, and Goethe, to Fichte, Hegel, and even to Nietzsche.[2] Furthermore, Fichte, Hegel, and Nietzsche were almost unknown to the masses. And as to Luther and Kant, it so happens that Hitler, Goebbels, Himmler, and Papen came from Catholic parentage, that is to say from an environment hostile to Luther and suspicious of Kant. Even the masses felt that the usurpers did not stand for Luther and Kant, and that there was no one less Goethean in the world than they.

Academic investigations of the intellectual origins of a movement should therefore not detract us from using other, and more suitable, methods to discover what the intellectuals and what the common people thought and believed at a certain time. The study of election campaigns and their results is most useful for this purpose. Such study may not reveal exactly which of the genuine ideas of Luther, Kant, and Goethe were still alive in Germany, or to what degree an inclination toward military ideals and discipline was still present even in the minds of workers. But they definitely show, as has been brought out in Chapter 1 above, that the overwhelming majority of the people at the end of the imperial period and during the democratic regime were distinctly anti-totalitarian and anti-fascist in both their ideas and their principles, and that this remained so at least throughout the 1920's.

[2] I should like to refer here to the profound article by Carl Mayer, 'On the Intellectual Origin of National Socialism' in *Social Research*, vol. 9 (1942), pp. 225-47.

Appendix B

The Weakness of Democratic Cabinets in Germany

The German Calamity: Disparity of Honest Views

GERMAN POPULAR OPINION WAS CERTAINLY NOT DEVOID OF common views. Any foreign visitor soon became aware of this fact. But most of the views held in common were negative in character. Thus people were practically unanimous in denouncing the Versailles Treaty and the thesis that Germany alone was responsible for the First World War. Until the later part of the 'twenties the vast majority were also at one in rejecting fascist doctrines and more than 80 per cent in opposing communist doctrines as well. When it came to positive views and constructive proposals, however, uniformity was lacking. Except on generalities such as love of country and of honesty, stressed by everyone—sometimes over-noisily —there was no agreement on positive fundamentals of any kind. The views held ranged from an uncomprising longing for monarchic restoration (with disagreements in regard to the candidates to the throne and the number of thrones to be re-established, whether federal only or state also) to socialist equalitarianism (with differences in regard to degrees and methods of socialization). A great variety of views filled the wide space between these extremes. Each of the groups had considerable strength. In fact, the political composition of the German people was so varied as to make it next to impossible on the basis of democratic procedure to form cabinets with a solid majority backing and capable of strong leadership. We must be careful to distinguish between this basic calamity, i.e.

the variegated political composition of the people, and the secondary one, that of a technical mistake in the Constitution, i.e. Proportional Representation for all elections. To integrate the German people by free elections into strong majorities would have been difficult under any electoral system. Proportional Representation made it practically impossible.

The detriment worked by Proportional Representation in several countries has been set forth with great skill in F. A. Hermens's classical manual, *Democracy or Anarchy?* [1] Suffice it to point here to the special unsuitability of this system for coping with the motley political opinions of the German people after the First World War. Under any method such as that used in the national campaigns of the United States and Great Britain, democratic elections would have confronted Germans in single-member constituencies with the alternative either of giving their vote to a candidate who had some chance of obtaining relative plurality in the district, or else of seeing their vote wasted. Voters would, therefore, have been forced to come to a *compromise* between their own views and those of others with whom they agreed on some essential points. On the other hand, victorious candidates, gathering their votes from people among whom were found a great variety of views, would have felt and behaved as the representatives of such a composite group. All this was fundamentally different under the German brand of Proportional Representation. Each voter cast his vote for any large or small group of his choice, and could be sure that it would be counted if at least 60,000 votes were given to the same group in a large region. Thus he was not being trained in the civic duty of peaceful integration. And each elected candidate felt and behaved as the stalwart representative of a compact group with common views.

[1] Cited in Chapter III, above. See also my review in *Social Research*, vol. 9 (1942), p. 411.

The many elements in the historical heritage that actually influenced the German people of that time were thus given *separate* expression. All those cleavages between monarchists and republicans, absolutists and constitutionalists, conservatives and liberals, authoritarian and equalitarian democrats, Protestants and Catholics, big business and labor, big and small farmers, Marxians and anti-Marxians, Marxians in favor of communist methods and those against them, were faithfully reflected and registered in the election results. So also was any shift in political views that resulted from the impact of defeat in the war, from occupation, inflation, deflation, reparation, disarmament, and unemployment. Elections recorded such changes in the shifting relative strength not only of two or three parties, but of fifteen or, if we include all those that competed in the elections without sometimes even reaching the requisite 60,000 votes, of more than thirty. There were separate parties and separate election results for each world view. This was paradise for statisticians, but hell for statesmen.

History in a Nutshell

The following simple facts illustrate the desperate situation caused by the varied political composition of the German people under Proportional Representation. They contain the history of the German Republic in a nutshell. The three parties of the so-called Weimar Coalition, namely, Social-Democrats, Liberals (Democrats), and Catholic Center, sincerely united in their support of a truly democratic system of government, obtained an ample majority early in 1919. Supported by this they brought about the adoption of the Constitution. If their coalition had continued in power, German democracy might have seen a healthy and stable political evolution—even, possibly, with Proportional Representation. Actually, however, the Weimar Coalition lost its majority in the Reich shortly after the acceptance of the Peace Treaty, in the elections of 1920, *and failed ever to regain it*. Hence no majority cabinet could be formed by this bloc again. Under normal democratic conditions thenceforth the parties to their Right might have formed majority cabinets. Yet these parties, too, never obtained majorities prior to 1933.

This fact, at first sight puzzling, finds its explanation in the existence of the anti-democratic Communists, who mustered enough seats to preclude the normal parliamentary play of governmental and opposition parties. They were only a minority, to be sure, never obtaining 20 per cent of the total seats. But their figures were high enough to disturb the balance of the parliamentary system. In the 7 elections from 1920 to '32 they obtained: in 1920, 4 seats (in addition to the 84 seats of independent socialists); 1924 (two elections), 62 and 45 seats respectively; 1928, 54; 1930, 77; July 1932, 89; and November 1932, 100 seats. They were certain to cast their votes against the Weimar Coalition as well as against the Rightist parties. The Weimar Coalition could therefore have formed a majority cabinet only if it surpassed the Rightist parties with a number of seats higher than that held by the Communists. It never did obtain so wide a margin after 1919.[2] Likewise, the Rightist parties were never able to form majority cabinets, because their margin over the Weimar Coalition, if any at all, was not large enough. This situation illustrates the unduly great power which some 'anti-everything' minority may obtain in a democratic legislature quite out of proportion to its numerical strength—a political phenomenon which has not yet received due attention.

There were then only two alternatives, if there were to be democratic governments at all. The one was to have a homogeneous minority cabinet, the other, to try out heterogeneous majorities. Minority cabinets could be formed either

[2] In Prussia it did—in 1928.

out of the members of the Weimar Coalition or of the Rightist parties. They would need support from day to day from
other parties in order not to be overthrown, and for this
reason would be weak despite their homogeneity. Eleven
such minority cabinets were in power for an aggregate of
eight years, that is for two-thirds of the period from 1920 to
1932.

Only for an aggregate of one-third of that period, i.e. for
four and a half years, did the other alternative materialize,
that of forming heterogeneous majority cabinets. To do so
one had either to add National Liberals to the Weimar Coalition and thus to combine the parties of big business and labor
in the same cabinet, or to yoke the pro-democratic and Catholic Center with the anti-democratic and Protestant German
Nationals. Both expedients were tried twice. Big business and
labor joined forces in the cabinets of Stresemann (August to
November 1923) and of Hermann Müller (June 1928 to
March 1930). Democratic Catholics and Conservative Protestants were combined in the cabinets of Luther (January to
December 1925) and of Marx (January 1927 to June 1928).
All four cabinets despite their respectable majorities were
necessarily weak because of the basic disunity of the com-
ponent parties in matters of immediate importance.

Political Weakness of Strong Personalities

German democratic statesmen have often been criticized
for their apparent weakness. It has not always been realized
that, owing to such conditions as described above, those willing to obey democratic principles of government were simply
pre-doomed to be weak, however gifted in leadership they
were and however strong they might have been under different circumstances. Take Stresemann as an example. He
was indeed a 'strong' personality, as strong as any democratic
leader could be. But how could he utilize his potential strength

in leadership, even during the period when he was backed by a majority, if that majority—including big business and labor as separate parties—was so precarious that he had literally to consume his strength fighting with his own party, or with others, for the mere purpose of keeping the majority together? Unless the 'strong man' was willing to overthrow the Constitution, or to use its loopholes to escape from parliamentary control, he could not but be weak in practice under the democratic rules of the game. No Churchill, Lloyd George, Clemenceau, Poincaré, or Roosevelt, whether Theodore or Franklin, could have run such a system in a vigorous fashion, unless—well, unless they were willing to transgress the limitations set by the Constitution. But from the democratic point of view, to do that seemed suicidal at a time when the attempt was being made to educate the people in loyalty to the fundamental law.

Proportional Representation vs. Integration

Let me repeat. It was essentially the diversified political composition of the German people rather than Proportional Representation which barred the way to strong democratic government. But Proportional Representation did prevent any attempt that might have been made to overcome that weakness by integrating diversified views in election campaigns. Great Britain with her single-member constituencies and relative-plurality campaigns could obtain large governmental majorities for more than twenty-two of the twenty-five years since 1918. Proportional Representation would have resulted in three-cornered fights in the Commons most of the time. Large majorities in the Commons made leaders even of doubtful strength appear strong, and made it possible to settle such critical problems as the general strike of 1926, the transition to protective tariffs in 1932 and the abdication of Edward VIII, and even to conduct Chamberlain's unpopular appeasement policy—all this with the appearance of strength and without seriously jarring the democratic system as such. Had Great Britain used Proportional Representation, her history would have been very different.

In the United States, the electoral system has kept fanatical minorities such as the Townsendites and Coughlinites, not to speak of Communists and Racists of all kinds, as separate groups out of the Congress.

Even the French parliament had at least the one great advantage over the German that absolute majorities or, in run-off elections, relative pluralities were required in single-member districts, so that local combinations of the constitutional parties could at any time outvote any anti-democratic or anti-parliamentary extremists of the Right or Left. They often did so. Accordingly, the French lower house had only a dozen Communists at a time when Proportional Representation would have given the Communists sixty or more seats. This difference was important as long as the Communists were still opposed to loyal co-operation with democracy, that is at least up to the formation of the Popular Front in 1936. No such local outvoting of extremists was possible under the German proportional system.

Appendix C

State Police Power and the National Socialist Party

IN ITS EARLY STAGES, FROM NOVEMBER 1922 TO DECEMBER 1924, the National Socialist Party was outlawed in Prussia. This action showed the vigilance of the Prussian democratic cabinet at a time when the semi-autocratic head of the Bavarian government, Gustav von Kahr, as well as his police president Ernst Pöhner, and the latter's aide in charge of political matters and thereafter head of Munich's criminal police Dr. Wilhelm Frick, granted the young National-Socialist movement ample freedom, the boundless use of which led up to the Munich Beer Hall Putsch of November 1923 (see above, Chapter 11). Only then did Kahr withdraw his protection, but Pöhner and Frick refused to obey him. They were arrested even before Hitler.

Pöhner's action offers a remarkable illustration to the ideology of leadership. I may insert a personal reminiscence here. In February 1921, praising the principle of unconditional loyalty to a personal leader, Pöhner asked me whether the Berlin republicans were willing to *die* for Friedrich Ebert, then President of the Republic. When I answered that the question for republicans was not whether to die for a man—that being their private affair—but for a cause, he taunted the republican form of government for such views. His leader was Kahr, he said, and he would die for him. That was, he added, the essential difference between his *Weltanschauung* and that of the republicans. Less than three years later, however, when his views differed from those of Kahr, he defied his former leader, ready to die not for but against him.[1]

A year later, 20 December 1924, the Bavarian cabinet used its quasi-sovereign state rights to pardon Hitler and his associates on the recommendation of Dr. Franz Gürtner, then Bavarian minister of justice. Gürtner became national minister of justice in Hitler's cabinet in 1933, Frick the first National-Socialist minister in one of the states, i.e. Thuringia, in 1930, and later national minister of the interior. Kahr, however, was murdered in the Blood Purge of June 1934. It was Dr. Gürtner again who offered the Reich cabinet the formula by which the executions without trial in that purge were legalized as acts for defense of the nation.

To come back to the early Prussian order, outlawing the National Socialist Party, this measure was based not on the strength of the general authority of the police to disband associations with illegal purposes, but on the Act of July 1922 for the Protection of the Republic. This federal act, passed immediately after the assassination of the foreign minister, Walther Rathenau, widened the authority of the police by clauses that contained concrete amendments to the Constitution and was adopted with the majority required for such amendments. Issued for five years and later extended for two more years, it expired in July 1929, shortly before the fascist movement began to attain greater importance. A new Act, of March 1930, for the Protection of the Republic restricted police action by fully restoring the general guarantees of individual rights as proclaimed by the Constitution. The

[1] Pöhner mentioned the discussion in the court hearings of 1924 to explain the principle of leadership, but he failed to add that it was Kahr for whom he said he would die. '*Und der König absolut wenn er unsern Willen tut*' (and the king ought to have absolute power provided he does what we want) as the views of many German monarchists have been interpreted. Pöhner died in 1925, so we don't know whether he would have been more steadfast in his personal loyalty to Hitler than he had been to Kahr.

political parties of the Right at that time refused to give the police any authority beyond these limits. The democratic parties, on the other hand, failed to muster alone the numerical strength to carry a constitutional amendment.

When the importance of the National Socialists was at its lowest, in December 1924, Prussia lifted the ban against the party. In May 1927, when violations of the law flared up in Berlin, the Prussian cabinet by virtue of the state's general police power disbanded the Berlin branch of the party, on the ground of its illegal purposes. This ban was maintained for almost a year, until March 1928. When the fight against Fascism grew more serious, in 1930 and 1931, the broader authorities granted in the first Protection Act had expired. The Prussian cabinet hesitated to outlaw the entire party or its storm divisions on the general ground of their illegal purposes. True, the Supreme Court, as illustrated by the decision quoted in Chapter x above, stated the illegality of the aims pursued by some National Socialist groups even after Hitler had sworn that he was only pursuing his goals legally. Nevertheless the Prussian cabinet did not feel confident that the Court would endorse the disbanding. The ministers rather feared that if the dissolution should be declared unconstitutional by the courts, and the storm divisions then could make their triumphant reappearance, matters would become only worse. The validity of the order would have been limited to Prussian territory anyway. Thus the cabinet preferred waiting for a presidential emergency decree disbanding the Storm Troops throughout the entire nation.

The present writer did not share the apprehensions of the Prussian ministers regarding the Supreme Court in this case. He was reasonably certain that at that time (1931) the Court would have confirmed the dissolution of the Storm Troops, and he thought that their disbanding on general grounds would be better than if based on Article 48 of the Constitution. This, however, was no more than a personal appraisal of the situation.

Special measures were taken for some time against Adolf Hitler himself, not only by Prussia but even by Bavaria. As a former Austrian and never naturalized in the German Reich, he was technically an alien. Aliens, whenever considered politically undesirable, could be banished from a states' territory irrespective of the constitutional principles that protected citizens. In 1925, when Hitler after being pardoned by the Bavarian cabinet engaged anew in his revolutionary campaign, both the Bavarian and Prussian cabinets forbade his making public speeches on pain of banishment. This ban remained inadequate, however, because some of the medium-sized states, such as Thuringia, Brunswick, and Mecklenburg, did not fall into line. Accordingly, Hitler could speak there freely and the newspapers could report his speeches everywhere in the country. Bavaria lifted the ban in March 1927. A year and a half later (September 1928) Prussia, too, dispensed with it, because sectional measures then restricted to Prussia were utterly inadequate; they merely exposed the Prussian cabinet to the charge of being afraid of the speeches of a man whom it could arrest whenever he violated a law. On the other hand, the National Socialists were rather weak at that time, for they had won only twelve seats in the Reichstag elections.

Finally Brunswick, in February 1932, went as far as to appoint Hitler a state official (*Regierungsrat*) for the mere purpose of effecting his naturalization. Under German law any foreigner became a citizen automatically upon his appointment as a civil servant to a federal or state office. Citizenship then entitled him to the full privileges of the democratic Constitution, including not only freedom of speech but also the right to become a candidate for the presidency.[2] Through this action of the small state of Brunswick with about 500,000 inhabitants, action against Hitler as an alien was made impossible for Prussia with her 40 million inhabitants.

These illustrations demonstrate the grave shortcomings in the Weimar Constitution, which, differing from that of the United States, made the federal government dependent for the enforcement of its policy on the different views of the several state governments. The Governmental Commission on Federal Reform (see Chapter vi) felt that these difficulties would only be aggravated if the Prussian police power were to be divided among the thirteen Prussian provinces, i.e. among so many more independent agencies of law enforcement. Divergencies such as those between Prussia, Thuringia, and Brunswick would be multiplied. The Commission therefore proposed that, after Prussia's elimination as an autonomous governmental unit, the supreme direction in police matters in Prussia should be exercised under parliamentary control by the central administration of the Reich rather than by the individual provincial governments. This should also be the arrangement for Thuringia, Brunswick, and the other minor states. The heads of the autonomous regional units in the provinces of Prussia and the medium-sized states were to obtain a great amount of freedom in their current police administration, especially in non-political fields, but subject to the ultimate direction of the national administration. Only Bavaria, Saxony, Württemberg, and Baden would retain their quasi-sovereign police power unmitigated.

[2] This is another illustration of the influence of constitutional details on the political history of a country. The democratic coalition in Weimar had failed to copy the American principle that only a person born in the country can become President. They omitted this qualification, ironically enough, with an eye to Austria, lest Austrians be excluded from the presidency merely because they were not born in Germany.

Appendix D

Constitutional Articles Involved in the Collapse of Democracy in Germany

THE TECHNICAL DEFECTS OF THE WEIMAR CONSTITUTION AND the attempts made to correct them have been discussed in Chapter VI and elsewhere in this book. The articles there referred to will be given below in the writer's translation. A few notes have been added. The excerpts do not include the articles regulating the federal system, i.e. the relation between the national government and the state governments.

1. *Proportional Representation.*
    Article 22 includes the following clause:

> 'The representatives [to the Reichstag] shall be elected . . . according to the principles of Proportional Representation . . .'

As to the implications of Proportional Representation see, in addition to Chapter VI the discussions in Appendix B.

2. *Dissolution of the Reichstag.*
    Article 25 reads as follows:

> 'The Reich President can dissolve the Reichstag, but he can do so only once for the same cause [*aus dem gleichen Anlass*].
> 'New elections shall be held, at the latest, on the sixtieth day after the dissolution.'

The President's right to dissolve the Reichstag has sometimes been condemned as a residue of authoritarian principles. Such general objection is, however, unjustified. The right was subject to the requirement of countersignature, as formulated in Article 50 (see below). A prime minister who has enjoyed the confidence of the popular chamber, or at least its active collaboration, may well obtain authority to appeal to the people if the majority of the house turns against him, or if he plans to engage in a fundamentally new policy. Such has been the traditional practice in Great Britain for almost two centuries. True, French parliamentary practice did abandon such dissolution after it had been abused by President Mac-Mahon in 1876. Yet there was in France a strong movement in the 1930's to re-activate this device under careful safeguards.

Safeguards were completely absent in the German Constitution. There was no certainty that the countersigning Chancellor might ever have enjoyed the Reichstag's confidence. On the contrary, the loose formulation of the clauses dealing with the Chancellor's appointment and with his right to stay in office until he suffered a vote of no-confidence (Articles 53 and 54, below) made it possible for the Reich President to dissolve the House on little more than his own authority alone.

Nor did the wording of Article 25 exclude repeated dissolutions. The very Reichstag returned by the elections after its predecessor had been dissolved could itself be dissolved, provided the President was able to refer to a 'new cause' for his decision. After all, it could be considered a 'new cause' that the new Reichstag was called 'even worse than its predecessor,' or 'unable to agree on a Chancellor and a policy,' or that it was faced with a new personal choice of the President, as occurred on 30 January 1933. See Chapters III, VI, VII and VIII on the role played by dissolutions under Article 25.

3. *Legislation by Decree. Suspension of Fundamental Rights.*
Article 48 may be translated as follows:

'(1) If one of the States fails to perform the duties
that fall upon it under the National Constitution or
under National Statutes, the Reich President with the
aid of the armed forces can hold [*anhalten*] such State
to the performance of its duties.

'(2) Whenever public safety and order in the German Reich are seriously [*erheblich*] disturbed or im-
periled, the Reich President can take any measures
necessary to restore public safety and order [*die
zur Wiederherstellung . . . erforderlichen Massnahmen
treffen*]; he may, if that should be necessary, intervene
[*einschreiten*] with the aid of the armed forces. To
restore safety and order, he may temporarily suspend,
in whole or in part, the fundamental rights as established
by the Constitution in the following Articles, namely,
Articles 114 [freedom from arbitrary arrest, prompt
judicial hearing], 115 [inviolability of the home], 117
[guarantees regarding secrecy of mail, telegraph and
telephone], 118 [freedom of speech and no censorship],
123 [freedom of peaceful assembly], 124 [freedom to
join associations] and 153 [guarantees regarding private
property].

'(3) The Reich President without delay shall inform
the Reichstag of any measures taken by virtue of the
above first and second paragraphs. At the Reichstag's
request the measures must be rescinded.

'(4) If there is danger in delay, any State government
may for its territory take provisional measures of the
kind described in the above second paragraph. At the
request of the Reich President or the Reichstag such
measures must be rescinded.

'(5) Details [regarding the subject-matter dealt with in this Article] will be determined by National Statute.'

The framers of this ill-fated article thought that any undemocratic abuse of it would be prevented by four safeguards. First, the President was to be elected by popular elections. Second, any measure taken by him required for its validity the countersignature by a person who had the Reichstag's confidence (Articles 50 and 54). Third, the measure had to be canceled whenever a simple majority of the Reichstag so demanded (Article 48, paragraph 3). Fourth, the Reichstag by simple majority could regulate further details (Paragraph 5).

All four safeguards, however, proved inadequate. Popular election of a President is no safeguard against the election of a person with authoritarian tendencies, especially in a country with authoritarian tradition. Popular outsiders, not connected with any particular party, have great advantages in presidential elections whenever Proportional Representation splits the legislature into many groups. See on this question Chapters II and VI, and Appendix B. The countersignature of the Chancellor proved to be no guarantee of parliamentary control because of the President's right to dismiss the Chancellor and to appoint another person (Article 53, below). The Reichstag's right to demand repeal was valueless if the Reichstag was dissolved (Article 25, above). The Reichstag's right to regulate details by special statute could not have healed the three other defects, because they were no mere 'details.'

Actually the Reichstag never passed even those regulations that it obviously was entitled to enact, such as a new version of the Protective Custody Act of 1916, which had become technically obsolete with the collapse of the imperial constitution. The reason for this omission was not mere negligence. It was rather because those parties that desired more elaborate safeguards refused to do piecemeal work for fear that they would lose the opportunity of pushing their more detailed proposals. They would, for instance, propose that any measure under Article 48 should go out of force automatically after three or six months. These tactics, together with the long abstinence from making any use of Article 48 between 1925 and 1930, led to the grave defect that not even the protection of individual rights as granted by the Act of 1916 had been re-enacted when Hitler came to power. See Chapter XI on the consequences of this omission.

Most references to Article 48 are to its second paragraph, dealing with dangers to safety and order irrespective of who was responsible. The first paragraph, more rarely referred to, concerns the special case of a state neglecting its duties towards the nation. Papen's proceedings against Prussia on 20 July 1932 were, however, based on both paragraphs. The Supreme Court expressly rejected the reference to the first paragraph, stating that Prussia in no way had failed in her duties towards the nation. See Chapter VII and Appendix E.

4. *Countersignature.*

Article 50 reads:

> 'All directions and orders [*Anordnungen und Ver-fügungen*] of the Reich President, including those relating to the armed forces, require for their validity the countersignature of the Reich Chancellor or of the appropriate Reich Minister. Through such countersignature responsibility is assumed [*übernommen*].'

No fault can be found with this article from the point of view of parliamentary democracy. Shortcomings followed, however, because of its connection with Articles 53 and 54 (see below).

5. *Appointment and Dismissal of the Reich Chancellor.*

The text of Article 53 is as follows:

> 'The Reich Chancellor and on his proposal the Reich Ministers are appointed and dismissed by the Reich President.'

This article was the main source of the trouble that arose from the articles previously quoted. Discussed and adopted at a time when a reliable adherent of the democratic form of government, Friedrich Ebert, was Reich President, it was formulated with little care for details. Obviously the framers had in their mind that appointment and dismissal should follow the principles of parliamentary democracy. But they failed to express their ideas clearly. The formula they chose made it possible for the President to dismiss a Chancellor for the sole reason that he, the President, had no confidence in him, and to appoint someone more amenable to the chief of state. He could safely do so, at least if he acted in good faith with a view to obtaining a majority in the Reichstag for his personal choice. Nor was there provision for limiting in any way the powers of a Chancellor thus appointed during the period between his appointment and the first meeting in which the Reichstag could express its confidence or the lack of it (Article 54, below). There was no indication either in Article 53 or in Article 50 that within this period the new Chancellor had no authority to countersign such important measures as that of dissolving the Reichstag (Article 25) or of issuing emergency decrees (Article 48). By making use of these loopholes, the President could obtain uncontrolled power for about two or three months. A newly elected Reichstag could finally assert itself against the President and his personal Chancellor, provided that majorities resulting from the elections were able to offer a candidate and a policy upon which they agreed. But three months of uncontrolled power are a long time under modern conditions and can easily be so used as to make any immediate re-establishment of a fully democratic government technically and practically impossible. See Chapter VII.

6. *Requirement of the Reichstag's Confidence.*

Article 54 read:

'The Reich Chancellor and the Reich Ministers need the confidence of the Reichstag for conducting their offices. Any one of them must resign whenever the Reichstag, by express resolution [*durch ausdrücklichen Beschluss*], withdraws its confidence from him.'

The second sentence of this article supports the interpretation that no Chancellor or minister, once appointed, need resign or in any way restrict his activities until the Reichstag had passed a vote of no-confidence against him. See the notes to Article 53 on the consequences of this interpretation.

Appendix E

Papen's Coup d'Etat of 20 July 1932

I

REICH PRESIDENT VON HINDENBURG'S DECREE OF 20 JULY 1932—proposed and countersigned by Reich Chancellor von Papen while general elections were pending, i.e. before the people through the Reichstag had any opportunity to express its lack of confidence in the Chancellor—read as follows:

Decree, Regarding the Restoration of Public Safety and Order Within the Territory of Prussia

By virtue of Article 48, paragraphs one and two, of the National Constitution, I ordain for the purpose of restoring public safety and order within the territory of Prussia, as follows:

SECTION 1

For the duration of this decree the Reich Chancellor is appointed National Commissioner for Prussia. In this capacity he is authorized to remove the members of the Prussian State Ministry [i.e. the Prussian cabinet] from their offices [*ihrer Ämter zu entheben*]. He is further authorized to assume the functions of the Prussian Prime Minister and to entrust other persons as national commissioners with conducting the Prussian Ministries.

The Reich Chancellor shall have all powers [*Befugnisse*] of the Prussian Prime Minister, and the persons entrusted by him with conducting the Prussian Ministries shall have all powers of the Prussian Ministers. The Reich Chancellor and the persons entrusted by him with conducting the Prussian Ministries shall exercise the powers of the Prussian State Ministry [i.e. the cabinet as a body].

SECTION 2

This decree shall go into effect with its promulgation.

Neudeck and Berlin, the
20th of July, 1932

The Reich President
von Hindenburg
The Reich Chancellor
von Papen

II

The decision of the Supreme Court for Constitutional Conflicts (*Staatsgerichtshof für das Deutsche Reich*) of 25 October 1932 was expressed in the following tenor, which in line with German judicial practice preceded the exposition of the findings and of the reasoning of the Court:

The Decree for the Restoration of Public Safety and Order within Prussia, issued by the Reich President on 20 July 1932, is compatible with the National Constitution in so far as it appoints the Reich Chancellor National Commissioner for Prussia and authorizes him temporarily to take away [*entziehen*] official functions from Prussian Ministers and either to assume these functions himself or to transfer them to other persons as national commissioners. This authorization, however, ought not to have been extended [*durfte sich nicht erstrecken*] to taking away from the Prussian State Cabinet and its members their power to represent Prussia in the Reichstag, in the Federal Council, or otherwise in her relations to the Reich, or in her relations to the Prussian Assembly, the Prussian State Council, or to other States.

In so far as petitions are not granted they are herewith rejected.

The Court was composed of seven judges, namely, the President of the National Supreme Court (*Reichsgericht*), Dr. Erwin Bumke, chairman; three justices of the National Supreme Court, and three justices of the supreme administrative courts of the states.

Appendix F

Excerpts from Ex-Chancellor Brüning's Letter
of August 6, 1944 to the Author[1]

Lowell House E-11
Harvard University
Cambridge, Mass.
August 6, 1944

Dear Dr. Brecht,

. . . I naturally read your book with very great interest, and I fully recognize and appreciate its tenor. It is very difficult at the present moment to create a better understanding of events in Germany after the last war [1914-1918]. . . .

I am always amazed that writers ignore the fact that the greater part of Germany's economic and financial and also international policy was dictated by the terms of the peace treaty. Nobody realizes that currency questions were under the legal sovereignty of the reparations creditors. While I was in office this sovereignty was exercised not only on general lines, but also in the details of the budgetary and monetary policy of the Reich. . . . Perhaps in a second edition you could include, for example, the fact that even a few days before

---

[1] The letter in its entirety is printed in Arnold Brecht, *Mit der Kraft des Geistes, Lebenserinnerungen zweite Hälfte,* Deutsche Verlags-Anstalt, Stuttgart, 1967, pp. 415 ff. Deutsche Verlags-Anstalt has kindly consented to the inclusion of these excerpts here.

Britain left the gold standard the British Ambassador brought me a note peremptorily demanding the further reduction of wages and salaries in Germany. It would also be important to mention . . . the law limiting the circulation of Reichsbank notes to a very low relation to the gold and foreign exchange reserve, of which you are aware. This might make people understand that the so-called deflationary policy was imposed on Germany. At all conferences it was made clear that the revision or cancellation of reparations would not be open to discussion unless the German government demonstrated that the greatest efforts within the frame of internal conditions laid down in the Young Plan did not permit the transfer of reparations. . . .

What strikes me even more in this connection is the fact that no German emigrant seems willing to study the consequences of our setting up a new Reichsbank—the *Akzept und Garantie Bank*—, which permitted us to make one of the largest credit expansions known, without which we would not have been able to survive the crisis of 1931. The technique we evolved was the model of every subsequent credit expansion. . . . The credits extended by the *Akzept und Garantie Bank,* together with the grant of Russian export credits, created within five months a total credit expansion of 2.500 million marks, without increasing the circulation of bank notes. We were the first to make a large-scale credit expansion, but in this way nevertheless remained within the legal restrictions of the Young Plan. . . . There is another point about which it would perhaps create a wrong impression for me to remain silent. . . . You seem to think that the use of Article 48 together with the dissolution of the Reichstag was a new interpretation of the Constitution and was responsible for the large increase in the Nazi vote. Any further postponement of the Reichstag dis-

solution would have increased the Nazi vote even farther. . . .
All our information from the country at large and my own
impression since the summer of 1929 convinced the Government unanimously that postponement of the election would
lead to disaster. We were not surprised by the results, as I
had calculated a possible 140 seats for the Nazis in the Reichstag.

Hermann Müller [Brüning's predecessor as Reich chancellor]
had promised Hindenburg to use Article 48 to carry through
the financial reforms entailed by the Young Plan. . . . It was
only after a year of struggle for any budget at all that President Hindenburg became aware of the dangers of the financial
evolution and refused to sign the Young Plan unless the
budget was balanced at once. In this situation Hermann
Müller pledged Hindenburg his word that he would introduce
necessary measures by Article 48, even against the opposition
of his own party, and risk elections. Discussions about the
constitutional aspect of the action . . . . were carried on by the
Hermann Müller Cabinet, including Zweigert and Joel [the
two chief governmental experts]. They agreed unanimously
that this measure was in complete conformity with the constitution. . . . When the SPD voted against the SPD ministers
. . . Hermann Müller called the Cabinet together and proposed
to use Article 48 and to dissolve the Reichstag if any difficulty
occurred. Then Meissner [Hindenburg's chief aide] inquired
of the President and reported that he would no longer give
Hermann Müller power to use Article 48 and dissolve the
Reichstag after his own party had voted against him. . . .
Without wanting to pester you any more, I will add only one
remark. The Center Party has never been a Roman Catholic
or clerical party. It has always tried to hold Protestant members, and in western and southern Germany it had from 7%

to 10% Protestant voters. The term Roman Catholic is very likely to be used further in abuse of me . . . our policy was entirely independent of any influence by the German episcopate or the Vatican . . . sharp clashes, such as that over the Concordat, frequently arose between the Vatican and the bishops on the one side and the Center Party on the other. . . .

Please forgive me for these remarks. My only aim, as I have said, is to present my point of view, as I feel it necessary to do in the face of a publication by a person of your position and qualifications, which I have always highly respected. . . .

Very cordially yours,
H. Brüning

Index